THE TIME
OF THE
BLACK JAGUAR

ARKAN LUSHWALA

Cover design by Carlos Guirados and Sophie Cooper

ISBN-13:
978-0615681818 (Arkan Lushwala)

ISBN-10:
0615681816

LCCN: 2012914582
Arkan Lushwala, Ribera, New Mexico

To order more copies of this book, please visit:
www.createspace.com/3953041

ACKNOWLEDGEMENTS

Many people have helped me through the process of writing and publishing this book. They are all dear friends and I thank them for their valuable contributions.

My deep gratitude goes out to David Tucker and the people of The Pachamama Alliance. I thank them for their dedication to preserve the rainforests and indigenous cultures of South America, and for their generous support in publishing this book.

I also want to acknowledge Cynthia Tunga Frisch for the beautiful way in which she helped me employ the correct use of the English language without compromising the authenticity of the voice of my culture.

CONTENTS

Forward

My brother writes with a vast knowing of history in Indigenous ways. His travels all over the world and his responsibility and commitment to keeping the fire of life going has brought him much insight and understanding of where we are to go as a human race. He does not tell you of all of the places he has been and of his own struggle to find balance within a world of abuse and neglect. He does not speak of the atrocities he has seen and the pain of ego that has been removed from his own heart. Instead, he talks of what we can do, where we can learn, and how we can save a planet that he so dearly loves.

His experience of what has been lost and what has been all along sits in his heart behind a deep love of our planet – our mother. And in his heart is an understanding of love that I have come to admire. In his heart is a feminine principle of that which flows, that which must flow – our sacred waters.

How is it that a white woman of Irish descent and a man of Peruvian ancestry come together as brother and sister in the North American Indian Country? Easy – we are of the same blood. We are of the same waters, we are of the same Earth, and finally we are of the same energy of the universe that is pure joy. We are love! This is a principle that our father Basil Brave Heart has taught us and so many others on the planet. These teachings of the heart come from individuals whose families have been wiped out by greed and the seeking of power. These teachings given freely without monetary payment are what lay in the center of the heartbeat of our mother the Earth.

My brother writes to you who are of this energy of love. You who are a daughter and a son of a planet we call Earth! You are our family. In this knowing, I implore you to hear what he is saying. It is not too late to save our waters. It is never too late to take care of one another and, in turn, to love this planet.

Arkan writes that in the separation of colors, the separation of genders, and the loss of communitarian life we can lose our heartbeat. In the *one single heartbeat* we find compassion – compassion for each other and compassion for all that is living. As he conveys his experiences of life and of ceremony, he discloses a way to understanding the simplicities of our elders and those who have gone before us. Within the hearts and minds of our elders, we find the balance necessary to move through these great times of change into greater knowledge of what is and what will be. He, like all spiritual leaders, has the key to joy held within his DNA and within his heart. As I read his words, I am taken to a place where I have been many times – a place that is in the heart of all human beings, a place where we all meet, the place of joy and understanding.

You may think that you are different than what he describes. You may be happy in your home and in your neighborhood right now. But will your children be happy with what you have left for them? Will your children's children be happy with no water to drink or sun to warm their faces?

I ask you to read every word, ponder each sentence that my brother from another country writes with all of his heart intact. It is in his words and in his message that we will find each other again as one heart, one love, and one single energy flow.

My brother talks of a word *haywaricuy* – which means to hand someone something with tenderness. I hand you this book with tenderness as a loving gesture to mankind, as sacred movement towards that which seems hopeless but is so easy to heal. We can come back together as one loving heartbeat for the good of all living things on this planet. For this, we need to recover our spirit. In spirit, there are no judgments, no words like hate or greed or mine or war. There are no guns; there is no destruction! Spirit will live on even if our precious Earth does not!

We are spirit, and my brother asks you to remember who you are, to wake up to the beauty that is, and to honor the beauty of life at all times just as your ancestors once did a very long time ago.

I stand next to my brother just as I support you in love! As Arkan says over and over: the essence of humanity can be one heartbeat, one movement of sacred direction! When we go against this direction we destroy. When we open to the spirit that we are and surrender to the sacred motion, then we prosper, we thrive, we love, and we live!

Thank you my brother for opening your heart to humanity!

JEANNIE KERRIGAN
Author of LAYLA, Spiritual Teacher and Founder of Ricky's Revenge Non-Profit

AUTHOR'S NOTE

Peru is Indian country, and since I was little I was fed by the wisdom of the ancient Andean culture. The memory that runs in the depths of the blood was always talking to my heart, helping me to recognize the spiritual value of the Indigenous ways. The ancient memory runs also in the rivers that are born in the tall snow-capped peaks of the Andes, and I grew up drinking this water.

Since a very young age, I chose to swim against the current. I was born in a country where most of those who had some of the blood of the white race would deny their Indigenous background and claim to be white and superior to others. I chose not to do this. I didn't believe in racial superiority and chose the opposite, to claim my Indigenous side. Far from wanting to take sides with one of the two races, what I wanted was to choose my path in life and my way of life. I had to make this choice in order to create peace within myself.

I had someone who came from Europe and a local Indian in my insides, always fighting for the territory that I am. This provoked chaos in the perception I had of myself and in my relationship to the world around me. These two parts of me had different inclinations and goals, and I was being pulled in opposite directions, sometimes feeling like someone who is falling without solid ground to hold me. Looking closely at them, I decided to love them both, but to have one guide the other – choosing the older brother so to speak, letting the wisest lead the way for both and for all the other parts of me.

I was a teenager the first time I went to look for my Indigenous Elders up in the Andean mountains, and they were waiting for me. It would have been enough to enjoy the warm feeling of being at home with the Indigenous people who welcomed me as family, fed me, and made me laugh and cry. But that wasn't all that they offered to me; everywhere I went, I was invited to learn the deepest sacred aspects of the ancient culture. Always encouraged by the Elders to participate in the spiritual rituals and ceremonies, I was guided to become one of those whose responsibility is to feed the continuity of the sacred traditions.

I want to clarify that I do not intend to create a separation between Indigenous and non-Indigenous people, for I believe that even though we are different, we are all the same. Neither do I want to make comparisons that could make Indigenous people look superior to other people. From what I know, based on my personal experience, Indigenous people do not have in their belief system any ideas of superiority over other human races or over any of the other forms of life on Earth.

Actually, what I feel when interacting with different types of people – and especially when sharing with them the ways of my ancestors – is that many people have the same conflict I had as a teenager: a conflict between the culture with which they have become identified and their indigenous side. I have felt this even in people who are pureblood white. They have shared with me how much they miss feeling indigenous to this Earth, how much they would love to be able to talk to the land and understand her language when she speaks to them.

I decided to publish this book because I believe that the heart of Indigenous people offers a reference for all human beings on the planet to remember their original nature – one that is compassionate, close to Nature, and capable of living cooperatively with others.

All of us, of all races and cultural backgrounds, have to choose between the path of cooperation and the path of competition. Because of our imperfection, we all have to always remember to choose a good path, a healthy way of life. For when we forget, we suffer and make others suffer. Of course, this has happened to Indigenous people too. History has examples of times when Indigenous people waged war on each other or abused each other. And still, these were the downfalls our ancestors had when overtaken by their shadow side. In their light, they have been able to keep alive, over thousands of years, a cultural thread based on a fierce determination to never loose the heart.

Nowadays, Indigenous people who are still healthy and rooted in the ancient wisdom normally choose the path of cooperation and beauty. Competition is seen as rude behavior that endangers the health of a community. The culture of cooperation reaches all relationships: not only between men and women, members of the same tribe and tribes with other tribes, but also between humans and all other forms of life.

We know from oral tradition that our first grandfathers were peaceful and loving people. Even during those times when some of their descendants experienced a spiritual downfall and engaged in brutal competition, others did not forget the heart of their ancestors. Many tribes and people within the tribes have continued following the ancient ways of the heart where the natural tendency is to cooperate with each other with humbleness and beauty and where kindness is the guiding behavior for all social relationships and the relationship with Mother Earth. Some of our Holy Men and Holy Women believe that the memory of these ways doesn't belong only to us, but to all of humanity, and therefore, I have permission to share it.

INTRODUCTION

When I was little, I felt bad when being told the story of the Three Little Pigs. Remember? One little pig builds a house made of straw and the wolf blows it down. The second one builds another house made of sticks, which are stronger than straw, and the wolf blows it down. Then the third little pig builds a house made of bricks and the wolf cannot blow it down. Tired of blowing, the wolf tries to get into the house through the chimney, and he gets captured by the little pig who cooks him alive in a pot full of boiling water that hangs over the fireplace. "Poor wolf," I thought at age five, when they told me this story in my first year of school. It was impossible for me to understand why our teacher thought the pig that built the brick house was the smartest, and why she wasn't feeling bad for the wolf. This simple story, which millions of children have learned for many generations, reveals a mentality, a social agreement, and points to a direction which apparently brings safety to humans but, at the same time, destroys Nature. Powerful industries have been developed all over the world so that humans can build the strongest buildings, roads and cities. All the resources needed by these industries are taken from the land and the waters of the Earth. In order to transport it all, powerful engines were invented. Trucks, cars and planes shaped the fast modern world, and Mother Earth provided, wanting or not, the fossil fuels that made them move. As if this wasn't enough, there have been many devastating wars to fight for control of the territories containing fuels and other natural resources.

According to how I understand it, the wolf in the story of the three little pigs represents the powers of the wilderness: the strong hit of the summer, the cold storms of the winter, the winds, the lightning, the lions, the snakes, and so many other wild powers which are considered to be a threat, sometimes to human safety, most times to human comfort. These are the wild powers that when put together as one single giant entity we call Pachamama; together they are the beautiful Egyptian Sphinx, the powerful Dragon; together they are balance. Looking for their safety, modern humans have treated the Earth in a way that broke Her balance, and this is the most unsafe thing to do.

This is why I don't think the pig who built the brick house is as smart as he believes himself to be.

It is evident that in modern times humans have believed in their capacity to rule over the Earth, building their sturdy "brick houses." And with their victory over the powers of Nature came a celebration consisting of "burning the wolf alive." This model of human life that destroys Nature at high rates will not be able to sustain itself for much longer. A cosmic time of renewal has arrived on Earth, and in order to be healthy again, Mother Dragon is putting all her parts back together.

Now with all we are seeing happening to the Earth, we are also seeing very sturdy buildings fall down and nuclear power plants leaking radiation. It has become clear that this mentality in which humans can defeat Nature and control the powers of the wilderness is based on an illusion, and probably on a certain sense of our own grandiosity.

It is the year 2011 when I am writing the last pages of this book. Just a few days ago a very strong earthquake and a tsunami hit the country of Japan. A country considered to have the third strongest economy in the world is now in a major crisis caused by the shaking of Mother Earth. Thousands of hours of work and disciplined effort made by the Japanese people since their last severe crisis in World War II came crashing down to the ground in only two minutes. Sacrifices made for so long, including the loss of time to enjoy life and to be with family and children at home, will not have their reward. Pachamama – Mother Earth, Mother of Timespace – took it all. Now I hear that because of the lack of electricity, some people are amazed at how many stars they can see at night. Because of the lack of food and water, people are feeling their heart open when someone unknown leaves some produce at the door of their semi-destroyed houses. For now, there are many who do not have to go to work, so they have time to gather in groups and talk to each other, tell old stories and remember how good it feels to have warm company, to be part of a tribe.

I wish the Japanese people would not have had to suffer so much, especially the children, the pregnant women, the elderly and all those who experienced the loss of their loved ones. There are times when things happen in ways that for us humans are difficult to understand. It seems to be that sometimes pain is needed in order for a change to happen.

Nonetheless, some changes are evidently necessary. I'm sure that I am not the only one who feels hope seeing that, because of these strong hits, we humans are remembering what is really important in life to the point of wanting to nourish and take care of it again. What are the Japanese people going to feel when they go back to work and try to rebuild the same world that proved not to be solid enough? Will they still feel that it is worth giving so much of their precious time to the rebuilding of such a world? Are there going to be people among them who will be looking for an alternative and doing things differently this time? I wonder.

Another story becomes possible when we humbly give thanks for our lives and for the beauty of this planet, and instead of "killing the wolf," we invite her to come in the house, offer her food, and sing her some of our heart's songs.

Recognizing the sacredness of her nature, we can develop a relationship of cooperation with the wild feminine being who gives us our food and water, who gives us all the beauty surrounding us, who gives us the storms and dangers helping us to stay awake. Our Indigenous grandfathers and grandmothers believe that it is from developing this respectful relationship that we can build a good world for the following generations.

It is time to re-write some of the old stories, and the Three Little Pigs is one of them. Imagine if in this story, as in many others, the wolf is not feared but, instead, treated as a wild friend, a teacher, and a partner. Imagine how the story goes when Pacha-mama, the wolf, and the pigs are one and the same life. It is time to write stories for the new tribes that will populate this Earth, visions that will be the foundations of a healthy world where humans are open in their hearts and relaxed in their bodies, free to be dedicated to add beauty to the beauty that already exists.

The purpose of this book is to share a mentality – the one carried by Indigenous people since ancient times – that has the power to make possible the conception of such new stories.

Because of the love we feel for all people and for Mother Earth, in difficult times when so much destruction is happening we can also see a world full of opportunities. Our heart seeks to awaken an expansive spiritual power – the sacred inner power that will enable us to cooperate with others and change what seems to be impossible to change.

Cosmic forces, Mother Earth, and thousands of awakened human hearts want to change everything and bring it back to its healthy state. This is a wave that will continue growing until it breaks in the shore of a new time. Nothing can stop it. It is life seeking to continue living. It is us seeking to continue living.

These pages are full of useful references for those who wish to take care of the Earth and the well-being of the following generations. They originate in ancient Indigenous cultures, especially the Andean culture of the place where I was born and the Lakota spiritual culture, which came to me as a gift and a blessing later in my life after moving to North America. The way I describe the wisdom of these traditions is the product of my personal experience. There are, of course, many others who could speak about the same subjects in different ways.

I want this work to be an offering to those who have questions about how to creatively participate in the change that is happening on Earth.

Indigenous people love making offerings to express their gratitude. Offerings have nourishing power. To nourish the ones who nourish us is what makes life continue. When we want to ask a sacred source to act on our behalf for something we need, first we offer it a gift. These pages are a humble offering to the sacred creative source that lives in the heart of the reader, your heart.

Before beginning to create, it is useful to remember the first story, the one that tells us who we really are.

1

THE MESSAGE OF THE EAGLE

It is well known that Indigenous people have a close relationship with animal spirits. For those who are not familiar with the deepest aspects of Indigenous cultures, I want to share that in truth we are not interested in worshipping animals. Our close relationship with them comes from recognizing that they are our relatives, that we share the same home, and also from the fact that many of them generously give their flesh to us so we may continue living. But most importantly, the relationship we have is with their spirit, recognizing that in their spirit they carry a sacred gift, a talent, and a "medicine" that is very helpful to us when we are open to receiving it.

In some of the following chapters, I will share experiences that I had in which I was deeply touched and guided by the medicine of some animal spirits like the jaguar, the spider, the snake, and the bear. One that we hold very sacred and that often guides me and my *tioshpaye* – or "extended family" in Lakota – is the Eagle Spirit. Eagle feathers are sometimes used in ceremony not just as decoration or because this is part of our folklore but to bring in the powerful help of the spirit of *Wambli*, the eagle.

We see you Grandfather Eagle. You belong to what is high, and still you have the capacity to descend and bring blessings to us. We thank you for your medicine, your unlimited vision that allows you to guide us when we are walking without being able to see where we are going. We thank you for the gift of direction and the sense of peacefulness that you bring to us from the spirit world.

When praying in this manner – to clarify for those who do not know our ways – in our mind, we are not talking to an animal but to a sacred power that is an aspect of the divine great power.

All creatures of Nature have a sacred gift; each one carries one of the sacred powers of the All. The eagle has the gift of being able to see far away, the owl has the gift of seeing in the dark and in all directions, the hawk has the gift of being brave. What about us? Are we a mistake of Nature or do we also carry a sacred gift? One time, after praying in a ceremony, the Eagle Spirit kindly responded to us. Wanting to help us remember who we are so we may live accordingly, he told us the story of where we come from.

This story, which refers to our first grandfathers, connects us to a time so remote that when talking about it we feel the flavor of a myth, and at the same time has so much to do with what is happening to humanity right now. The best direction for us to take becomes clear when we remember who we are, and I believe this is why Grandfather Eagle gave us this gift.

This is what I remembered that he said:

"In the beginning there was only a point of light. This point of light fused its feminine and masculine energies and exploded, generating seven stars. All at once, these seven stars also fused their masculine and feminine energies and exploded, generating the thirteen creators of this world, who manifested the existence of all beings through their singing and dancing.

"The thirteenth, conducting the dance, was the one who had maintained his duality intact within himself: Eagle Dancer. To his left were six female dancers, and to his right six male dancers. They formed a circle standing on top of the open space of nothingness, each one of them carrying a staff with which they banged on the floor of nothingness calling it to become something. The first thing to appear before them was a tree that was an animal.

"While the dancers of Creation continued with their movements and songs, fruits began to appear in the branches of the tree, which are now all the animal species and all the plants that reside on Earth. One by one they detached from the tree and found their place on the terrestrial space that the dancers had called to solidify itself from nothingness. In this way the world and its inhabitants were created.

"At the end, the dancers who sang the Creation of the world decided to leave a species on Earth that had qualities similar to those of themselves. They created women and men and left them with the mission to care for the rest of Creation through the power of their heart and their capacity to produce refined vibrations. The first humans were born to be guardians of the memory for the original design of life, guardians of the memory that resides in the song and dance of Creation. Keeping this memory alive in their heart and singing it back to all that lives became their gift, their mission, and the foundation of a beautiful way of life.

"Over time, the giant and powerful humans grew in numbers. Enjoying the fruits of their intelligence and their creative capacities, they kept life in balance and made beautiful things with what the Earth gave them. Some kept living in simple tribal ways while others developed great civilizations that became containers of universal wisdom.

"When they were at the peak of their power, darkness showed up in the souls of many, and for the first time humans knew emotions like jealousy, envy, and greed. Those trying to prove to be the most powerful and beautiful among the rest competed with each other and, in doing so, ended up wounded. A strange kind of pain related to the loss of unity with others, which came together with the loss of oneself, gave birth to fear. Defensive and aggressive behaviors born from fear made them close their hearts.

"Disconnected from the radiant light of their spirits, they kept going further away from their original selves. With time, they forgot their origin and the way Eagle Dancer encouraged them to sing in the beginning, becoming one. Those who had grown a hole in their souls had a craving for becoming *the one*, ignoring that *the one* is really *the one heart* that is born from cooperating with others. The original brotherhood of the humans got lost. Some nations developed strong ethnic identities that they used for stating that they were not like the rest, forbidding their young ones to marry with an outsider.

"When the humans became divided, the rest of Creation lost the contributions of its caretaker. Their violence made them hurt not only each other but the Earth as well. The balance of life became debilitated to the extent that the Tree of Life became ill and began to die; its withered branches fell upon the Earth generating earthquakes, volcanic explosions and flooding.

"This violent way of life continued until one day when some of them decided to climb to the top of a mountain to cry for help. They were the ones who, listening to the beating of their own frightened hearts, remembered the staffs of the dancers of the Beginning, banging and banging, calling life.

"On the mountain their vision was healed and they remembered themselves, being able to feel their hearts again. When they came down they knew what to do. The dance and songs of the beginning were once again offered to the Tree of Life, which now was a dying tree. Fallen branches were good for making drums that made the heartbeat of the Tree of Life resonate throughout the Earth. The branches were also good for lighting the sacred fire that showed them the spirit of the Tree. In front of this Tree they danced to the rhythm of the drum day and night, elevating their vibration higher and higher. In alignment with the beginning and the origin of all things, remembering and healing themselves, they were able to re-establish the health and equilibrium of life on Earth."

I consider this story that we received from Grandfather Eagle to be extremely important, because it tells us what we originally are, that we are capable of forgetting, and that we are also capable of remembering.

I find a story like this infinitely more useful than those that lead us to believe that we human beings are originally destructive and competitive killers who need to be educated in order to have a good heart.

Not only has religion told us that there is something inherently wrong with us; modern social sciences have told us this as well. Official books of social sciences repeatedly state that war is what determines the development of civilization. With statements like this one, we have been lead to identify ourselves with our destructive side – and that with which we become identified, we overvalue and empower. This has been happening for many generations, reinforcing this harmful image of ourselves.

2

THE TRUTH HIDDEN
UNDER THE SAND DUNES

When I was a child, during the summers, I went to my grandmother's house in the humble fishermen's village of Caleta Vidal on the coast of Peru. By then, we already knew that we were surrounded by pre-Incan cemeteries, mostly from the Chancay pre-Incan culture; we often found ancient pieces of tapestry and ceramic under the sand as well as bones and skulls. But just recently, my family became aware that grandmother's house was sitting on a land that in remote times used to be part of the area of the ancient Caral civilization. A couple of miles away from the fishermen's village, eight pyramids were excavated just a few years ago, and when they finish excavating, there will be a total of thirty-two pyramids.

Recently, I returned to my grandmother's house after twenty-five long years. Something felt different in the house now that Grandma had gone back to the stars, but mostly everything looked exactly as I had left it since my last visit. The adobe walls were still decorated with marine landscapes from all over the world that my aunts had cut from magazines. The same old bedroom was waiting for me at the end of the house, but now it seemed smaller than how I remembered it. Wondering how so many children used to fit in such a small room, I fell asleep smiling, surrounded by the sounds and smells of the best times of my childhood.

A very strong dream arrived in the middle of the night. It was nighttime in the dream as well. From a big fire placed in the center of a stone altar, ancient Indigenous people moved towards me like shadows. One of them was an old woman, calling me, inviting me to come closer. Then, I abruptly woke up, and half asleep, walked with the help of a flashlight directly to a room in the house that was being used for storing very old furniture – and there was Juanita!

My grandfather used to go to the sand dunes some nights to find old pieces of pottery, and one morning he came back home with a skull in his hands. He said it belonged to a woman and called her Juanita. He and Grandma decided that from then on she would be the guardian of the house. I was very surprised when my flashlight spotted her skull. It felt so good to see her again. I remembered being afraid of her when I was little; but now that she had showed herself in my dreams and woken me up in the middle of the night, I was thrilled and happy. I accepted the invitation received in my dreams, and the next day took off towards the pyramids and ceremonial spaces of the ancient Caral nation.

Thanks to a very kind local gentleman who was hired to work with the archeologists and served as my guide, I quickly understood what my eyes were seeing. Essentially, the Caral people, as ancient as the Egyptians, were "people of the beginning," our first grandfathers in South America who did not know war.

I was very impressed to hear that at Caral no weapon has ever been found by the archeologists. I was also relieved now that the truth had emerged from those old sand dunes. Instead of weapons, what they found by the hundreds were musical instruments, with lots of one tone flutes among them. Finally, the truth that I always felt was revealed in front of my eyes: the old scientific theory that says war is what determines the development of a civilization was proven to be wrong. Music, on the other hand, as the art of elevating vibrations and putting them in the air so they may go everywhere and nourish all beings, was essential for those from whom we originally descend. The pyramids, sacred fireplaces, and all the powerful ceremonial spaces of Caral were the sacred containers for the thousands of souls who played the instruments and created the vibrations. Imagine them, thousands of people all together under the stars, the fires lit in the temples that surrounded them, sending the sounds of their flutes out to the Universe.

It is commonly known by Indigenous people that high-frequency vibrations activate consciousness, nourish what is hungry or weak, heal what is sick, and invite in the most luminous forces of Nature. Because of my experience with Indigenous sacred ceremonies, it became clear to me that the main focus in the minds of the Caral people was taking care of all that lives. They did not see themselves as conquerors or competitors; they saw themselves as caretakers of life. Our first grandfathers, far from being interested in greedy conquering ventures, were occupied with adding beauty and power to the beautiful Earth that gave them their bodies and the food and water that nourished them. Considering that they did not have any defensive structures or weapons, they must have always been open in their hearts and willing to share with others what they had. Therefore, I believe their economic system was based in generosity and reciprocity, as it still is nowadays in many Indigenous communities. With generosity and reciprocity, they took care of all living creatures without exception; their heart following the good example of the rains that fall on everyone and of the Sun that doesn't exclude anyone from receiving its light and warmth.

In Peru, a *waka* – such as Caral, Chavin, or Machu Picchu – is a sacred place, a center of spiritual power and of ancestral memory. Some *wakas* are hundreds of years old, and some, like Caral, are many thousands of years old. When my cousins and I were little, we had many places where we could go and play, but I always liked to go play in a *waka*. Something invisible that lived there made me feel peaceful. It was exciting to suddenly find a piece of old pottery or a piece of pre-Incan tapestry, and right away start imagining the people who lived there so long ago. When I was old enough to travel by myself, I started going to Cusco and to other locations along the Andean mountain range where I visited many beautiful *wakas*, Machu Picchu among them. Back then, there weren't that many tourists, so I could stay for a long time in the temples, walk in silence, pray, and receive the memory and instructions that our ancestors left recorded in the stones.

When you sit quietly and long enough staring at one of the stones that our ancestors shaped and carved, eventually the stone starts *talking* to you. In some way, it shows you the world that the ancient people saw through their eyes. What a magic world that was! Our ancient grandfathers had a mind very different than ours; their mind was really free and wise, naturally connected to the sacred motion of the cosmic forces. They built a world on Earth which was like a mirror where the cosmic dance could reflect itself and resonate, and where all beings could receive the nourishment of this vibration.

When seeing the remains of ancient temples in places like Egypt, Guatemala, Peru, and many others, it is evident that the work of creating these *sacred mirrors* to produce and freely share high-frequency vibrations was extremely important to them. The amount of effort they put into this task can be easily appreciated. Nowadays, someone might say that this was part of the artistic and mystic veins of the ancient ones, and that hunting and growing food to have a strong economy must have been their priority;

but it wasn't. What today may be considered art or mysticism, for the ancient ones, was crucial for the sustenance of life.

3

SUN, LIGHTNING, VOLCANOES AND HUMANS

In the ceremonial community where I now live and pray in northern New Mexico, there is a small fountain with water that is the door of life. It is there to honor all the feminine waters, the wombs of all women and female animals as well as the womb of Mother Earth and Her nourishing power that keeps us alive. At night, it is a mirror where the moon and the stars can see themselves. This fountain is right in the middle of the area where people usually gather, right in front of the kitchen and dining building.

More than once I have found the footprints of wild animals that come at night to drink from this fountain. One time, I even found the big footprints of a mountain lion. Throughout the years, I have been able to observe that they come to this water altar more often when there are more people. At first, this didn't make sense, but then the obvious became clear to me: the times when there are more people are usually the times in which our sacred fires are lit and we are having a ceremony. They feel the vibrations of our ceremonies and feel safe approaching the areas where we live at those times. Somehow, they know that they will not get shot. They can feel that when we pray, we are praying for them too.

One time, doing a ceremony at a forest in New Hampshire near the east coast of the United States, I had the chance to learn much about the power of vibrations. We had lit a fire to make an offering to the spirit of a beautiful mountain called Mount Monadnock and to all the creatures and spirits of the forest. With the help of my rattle, I was singing and singing but did not get the immediate response that I usually receive when singing to the spirits of Nature. I felt a great emptiness in my soul when, after singing for a while, nobody responded. In the mountains of South America where I come from this never happens, so I got a little scared and confused. But I kept singing and calling.

I could feel that there was a bear living in that area, so I started singing to him until he appeared. It was a really big black bear, walking in circles behind the tree line that marked the boundaries of the clearing where we were sitting. Somehow, one of those rare things that happen in ceremony happened that day. The rest of the people who were there could not be aware of this, but I was listening in my mind to the thoughts of the bear. He was suspicious of us humans, because nobody had come to sing and make offerings in that forest since the Indians were massacred a long time ago. In a very humble way, I cried with my song, asking him for forgiveness, telling him the good news that the white people who were there with me wanted to keep coming to this forest in the future to sing and make offerings. I asked him to use his powerful medicine and help me to awaken the spirit of the forest, and he did so.

After this, the feeling completely changed, and the spirits of the forest started coming to receive the offering and to dance with the vibration of our songs and prayers. Everyone there noticed the change. What a relief! For many years now, some of the people who were in that ceremony have kept their word and continued going to the same spot at the change of every season to light a sacred fire and make offerings to Mount Monadnock.

Since ancient times, the other life species have seen and recognized that humans are the only earthly creatures who can light a fire, and that we share this sacred capacity with the sun, the lightning bolts, and the volcanoes. In the remote past, this quality earned us the love and respect of the creatures and spirits of Nature. Now we are mostly feared. Throughout modern history, man-made fires used for war have so many times destroyed entire mountains, forests, and cities that were not only the homes of humans but also of many precious life forms.

Lighting sacred fires has to do with our necessity to open a door, the mouth of Spirit, the mouth of Pachamama, in order to give nourishment to the sources of life. This is a serious responsibility, much less romantic than it seems. When forgetting to nourish the forms of life that nourish us, everything begins to decay and lose its radiance. Keeping life in balance is an art that comes from the most sacred wisdom received by our grandparents, wisdom still alive and practiced by many Indigenous nations around the world.

The enchanting tribal worlds where these arts are practiced are getting smaller and smaller. The high-tech, high-speed modern world and its global economy is a continuously growing giant. Humankind has consumed millions of tons of resources taken from the planet during the last decades, pushing many forms of life to the verge of extinction. In this modern society, there isn't any consistent practice or tradition used for compensating the Earth for all that is taken from Her. There are no social habits directed to returning energy and beauty to the big "holes" that are left after resources are cut, gathered and consumed. Mostly, a minority of Indigenous people of different nations around the world are still lighting the sacred fires from which the spirits of the mountains, the forests, the rivers and the lakes are nourished.

In the Indigenous worlds still alive, we have never stopped lighting the ancient sacred fires. When a fire is lit in order to sing, dance, and pray, these vibrations resonate over all of Creation. The continuity of life is fed by the ceremonies that we do at the important cosmic dates – those days when all is open and aligned. We humbly feed the fire, sending nourishment to the spirits of the mountains, to the *thunderbeings* that give us the rain, to our father sun, to the four-legged masters that always share their wisdom with us, to the grandmothers that crawl, and to the magic beings that swim in the ocean. We feed the spirits of the plants that nourish and heal us and the animals that give their lives so we may eat their flesh and continue living. We put medicine in the wind, in the water, in the fire and in the earth, and our medicine travels to every place where it is needed. We make sure to do this with beauty and grace – wearing colorful clothes, with refined singing and dancing, with the joyful participation of the community. We are careful to do it all from our heart, allowing the Great Mystery to conduct us and to make us say and do wonders that contribute to the creation of a good life for everyone. The results of our prayers are always good, but the merit is not ours. The only thing we do is to participate in the cosmic dance with the best we have, and the universal sacred powers are the ones who do the main work.

The Indigenous Elders of the world in which I was born say that when we stop nourishing that which nourishes us, removing ourselves from the cosmic dance that generates life, our world becomes ill and eventually comes to an end. Andean people, like most Indigenous people around the world, have in their traditions ways of making offerings to nourish Pachamama, our Mother Earth. In the Andes, we use the word *ayni* to name the art of reciprocity. *Ayni* is an essential aspect of Andean culture. It manifests in great offering rituals as well as in simple gestures of gratitude toward those who are part of our life. For everything that one receives, there is something to give in return. In our *despachos* or "payments," which are our ancient ceremonies of reciprocity, we offer to the Apukuna – the spirits of the mountains – and to the heart of Pachamama something similar to what we are requesting. When asking for rain, for example, we add to our offering small cotton balls that become clouds through our prayer's breath.

It would be rare in the Andes for someone to build a house without first giving payment to Mother Earth. This payment is a beautiful, colorful, and scented offering of food, coca leaves, and powerful prayers. The vibration of what is put in the offering nourishes the land from where the materials are taken to build the house. To make payment, in this case, is not a mechanical action, like when we comply with a mandatory fee. It is an action that comes from the heart.

A Runasimi or Quechua word of the Andes used to describe what in other cultures is understood as payment is *haywaricuy*, which means "to hand something to someone with tenderness." After all, this is what makes us humans: our deep desire to hand a gift to the sources of life, through the smoke of our offerings and with the beauty of our prayers and songs.

Every day, we receive food and water. Every day is a good day to nourish and to keep in good health the sources of our nourishment, giving them thanks with power words, beautiful creative words that today we call prayers.

4

THE POWER OF
GIVE AWAY CEREMONIES

My older brother gave me many examples of
generosity, for which I deeply thank him, along the
many years that he guided me through the Vision
Quest path. As is common among our people, I gave
him tobacco and a gift when asking him to put me
on a hill where I could stay alone fasting and praying
for several days and nights. Since he was going to
take care of my life, I made sure to give him
something really useful, no matter how much it cost,
and he was always happy to receive it. More than
once he told me that in some way he would make
good use of the gift. Time after time, the destiny of
these presents was always the same: later, I saw some
other person using what I had given him. He gave
away every present he received from me, and
sometimes he gave me presents that others had given
him. "This is really good!" I concluded one day. It
was just the natural expression of his wisdom and his
big heart. He didn't let anything stay stuck in his
hands; he made sure that everything kept *circulating*.

The Lakota people have a very beautiful way of calling that which in many religions people name God. I learned from my *Ate* (father) Basil Brave Heart to pray calling *Taku Wakan Skan Skan*, which means "Something that is Sacred Energy in Permanent Motion." This sacred motion is what my older brother and all the Elders on my path have taught me to feed with my prayers as well as to call upon when great help is needed. This energy is what they say has to always be circulating, moving in small and big circles, for all life to always stay alive and full of the original vitality of the light of Creation. In this sense, our acts of generosity and reciprocity are not just things we do for people to see how good we are; they are really about assuming our share of responsibility in feeding the health and continuity of life.

All Indigenous healers and also the common people know that illness is the product of some energy that got stuck. When ceasing to flow, it lost its vitality, its nourishing power, becoming the opposite: some kind of black hole that sucks all the energy around it destroying life. Therefore, it wouldn't be strange for an Indigenous healer or ceremonial leader to see greed and the incapacity to share as illnesses. Any human attitude that prevents the universal energy to circulate freely is creating illness. And I understand someone may say without bad intention that the energy of their not-shared wealth belongs to them because they or their parents worked hard to earn it; but, in a sense, there is simple ignorance in this point of view: all energy is universal. Even the energy that gives us the talent to create our wealth is universal. In our last hour, it will be taken from our bodies so it may be put back into circulation in the great circle of life, while our bodies go underground to feed the Earth.

To honor this universal energy properly and keep ourselves from falling into the path of ignorance, Indigenous people often do *give away* ceremonies.

The traditional *give away* ceremonies, which in the Lakota tribe are called *Wopila* – meaning "gratitude" – are to my taste the simplest and most beautiful. In these ceremonies we find the opportunity to not be attached to our belongings, letting go of that which we are beginning to believe is ours. *Give away* ceremonies are the ones in which we strengthen our trust in the Great Spirit and Mother Earth. Sharing with others, we let go of our belongings with the spiritual trust that we are always given what we need.

The practice of *give away*, according to how I understand it and how I interpret what I have seen, reminds us that we do not want to be those who block the flow of the universal energy, which is meant to always be in motion. Sharing from the heart is what makes this motion stronger. For those Indigenous people who are still free and uncontaminated by the consumerism of the modern world, accumulating belongings is contrary to what makes them feel good. It doesn't feel good to stop anything from circulating and being part of the natural flow of life. It feels good to share, to be fire that gives a boost to the natural flow, to be water that offers itself to those who are thirsty. Those who visit the homes of Indigenous people or who spend time living with them know this for a fact: it doesn't matter how little food a family has – they will always share from their heart with anyone who comes to visit.

I remember when my little sister Marilyn did her first *give away*, to express her gratitude for having completed four years of Vision Quest ceremonies. As is customary, after coming out of a sweatlodge ceremony she fed all the people and then laid a blanket on the floor with many beautiful things on it for people to take. But this being her first time, she just thought about buying what she could in the store – little things that would make people happy. And yes, we were all happy. But then she grew up, learned more, and when she did her second *give away* ceremony, what she put on the blanket were her own belongings, things that she really needed and knew would be useful to others. She pretty much gave away all her clothes. Talking about this with her just recently, she told me that since the day of that *give away* ceremony, she is surprised to see how much clothing she keeps receiving; people are always gifting her all kinds of nice skirts, blouses, and jackets.

Our ancestors were always observing Nature and the influence that we humans have in Nature. They wanted to know, for example, how human actions could have an influence on the arrival of a drought, and from watching they learned. When goods harvested from the Earth or energy given to us for free by the Cosmos stop circulating freely, the circle starts vanishing, the great circle of life becomes weak and ill. As a result, many forms of life that are part of the circle experience a lack of what they need to sustain their lives, and the world we live in is impoverished. At the end, the circle where vital energy flows seeking to nourish all living creatures is replaced by a man-made vertical structure in which those at the top have more access to the goods than those at the bottom. In this structure, everyone has the potential of getting sick – those at the top for having too much and those at the bottom for not having enough of what is necessary.

When giving away our belongings, we don't really lose them. This is an act of power that feeds the motion of vital energy in the great river of life, making it stronger, so there are always rain and food for everyone. At the end, all that we let run on the river sooner or later comes back to us like a rain of blessings.

HALLOWEEN

Talking with some friends about the celebration of Halloween, I understood it as a version of a *give away* ceremony originated in pre-Christian Europe. My friends explained that in the original design of Halloween, the children in costumes represent the spirits and the people whose homes they visit feed them with candy as a ritualistic way of "feeding the spirits."

I can see that today there still is a massive give away of candies and chocolates on Halloween, but the original design of this celebration seems to have suffered many changes throughout the centuries. I heard that a major change happened in Europe when religious authorities prohibited rituals considered to be pagan, and only a few brave women, at the risk of being burned alive, dared to continue to feed and give thanks to the spirits. The Halloween ritual began to be seen as a day of witches and ghosts, and its sacred side fell into oblivion. Still, religious prohibition could not actually eradicate the people's need to have a day in which to celebrate and to feed their dead. So, with its dark and pagan stain, the tradition remained alive for centuries.

Even though some European and North American towns succeeded in the ritual's survival despite the religious prohibition, they were unable to resist the effect of its commercialization. The loss of profundity is always the effect of commercialization in Halloween, Christmas, and many other celebrations that originally required that people participate with their whole heart.

Today Halloween is no longer a celebration whose form and character are born from the hearts of the people; today they are born from the creative minds of marketing managers and publicists who work for large corporations that sell chocolates, caramels, costumes, and plastic pumpkins.

Halloween is not celebrated where I was born like it is in North America. However, I did know that on the evening of the 31st of October, people put on costumes, paint faces on pumpkins, and children walk through the streets knocking on doors to receive candy and chocolates. When I later came to live in New Mexico, I could witness the celebration more closely and understand it better, most of all by observing my daughters and their friends. I saw some of the children looking like real devils as they carried sacks full of candy and chocolates, feeling that they did not have enough, arguing over who had the most, and not having any desire to share. It bothered me to see the faces of those little ones possessed by a kind of insatiable ambition. This is why I spoke with my daughters, asking them to be conscious should this ambition ever be present within them as they join in the fun and share in the joy of Halloween with other children.

After one Halloween night, my daughters returned to my house and told me that after going through the streets dressed as sinister creatures, they sat down at a table with other children to proudly show each other the candy they had harvested. A girl with them named Anna not only showed off her great harvest, she also circulated the bag full of candy among the children so that each one could take from it whatever they wanted. After doing this, she had no candy left. Back at home, my children could do nothing else but talk about what Anna had done.

I can see that the celebration of Halloween is very similar in origin to the ceremonies we do in the Andes to feed the spirits or the ones done in Mexico and many other places on the Day of the Dead. Each culture creates a different way of doing it, but the purpose of these ceremonies accomplishes the same thing. As the heart of little Anna knew, the purpose of this and many other ancient spiritual ceremonies is to nurture that which and those whom we love. Feeding the spirits and having a day to remember the dead is something serious and sacred. It is also part of the practice of tribal economy born simply from the talent that we have as human beings to feed that which and those who are hungry, keeping all life in good health and equilibrium. I strongly believe that this talent shows our real nature; it is part of who we are, just like little Anna demonstrated in spontaneously giving away her chocolates to the other children.

THE LACK OF INTELLIGENCE IN MODERN ECONOMY

Unfortunately, the modern economy that led to the globalization of the world markets is not run by people like little Anna. On the contrary, it wouldn't survive without promoting greed as a high quality that leads to success. Modern economy contains an ambitious aspect that makes a few entrepreneurs take even the most authentic and beautiful of what the people create and convert it into a source of profit. In this sense, what happens to celebrations like Christmas and Halloween is just one of the thousands of possible examples showing us what the modern economy is based on – the creation of profit at the cost of damaging the source of the profit.

When the source of profit is a traditional costume of the people, then the authenticity of the custom is damaged; when the source of the profit is a forest, then the forest is damaged; when the source of the profit is a mountain, then the mountain is damaged; when the source of the profit is the sea, then the waters are poisoned; when the source of the profit are the laborers who are also the consumers, then their health, freedom, and tranquility are damaged. We do not have to be overly intelligent to become aware that this system is condemned to self-destruct. Where will the profits come from the day that all the sources run out? How can an economic system sustain itself in which its sources for profit are constantly destroyed?

Looking at it with simplicity and without judgment, it is very foolish, not very intelligent, to destroy the source of profits that sustain the economy. Mother Earth, the source, is being destroyed in a short amount of time by supposedly the most intelligent civilization that has ever existed. Beautiful traditions for sharing and nourishing that used to remind us humans of our big heart are being destroyed at the same rate.

A civilization that turns an ancient *give away* ceremony with the power to keep life in balance into a business that creates fun and profit for a few is, from my point of view, falling down the path of oblivion. And this puts us all in danger.

5

A Sacred Economy

After our grandfathers were "conquered," the authorities decided that we had to go to school in order to become good citizens of their world. When doing this, they didn't take into consideration that we needed time to continue being trained in the loving life arts. Those who destroyed our ancient sacred spaces didn't know that from these temples we watered their food as much as ours. Without really knowing what they were doing, they took the gold we were using for the generation of highly refined energy. It was sad to see gold, which for us was the most visible manifestation of the Sun's radiant generosity, become a matter of greed.

They also took the lands where our grandparents lived and declared that now these lands were owned by them. The survivors of the struggle were offered a slave job in exchange for keeping their lives. Our brothers who came from the other side of the ocean were never satisfied, no matter how much they possessed. Despite all their knowledge and the good tools they brought, they didn't really know how to take care of the Earth in a deep way. To have a reciprocal relationship with Pachamama was not part of what they knew. Seeing that they couldn't keep life in balance, we were determined to continue doing our spiritual work, even when their Church severely punished us for doing so.

Andean people, like most tribal people of this continent, have never stopped calling the Earth "our Mother," not even when people showed us those legal papers that said She belonged to them. There were prohibitions and punishments for those who celebrated the ancient rituals, and yet, throughout the centuries, we managed to continue lighting the sacred fires in so many different corners of the big temple that is Pachamama. How could we live without praying and giving thanks? We have the chance to continue being real human beings as long as we continue nourishing the sources that nourish everyone; this is true even for the children of those who took the land by force. No one is excluded from our prayer. If we excluded anyone, then our prayer would not be real, and we would be ignoring what we learned: that no matter how we act, we are one. This is how tribal economy works – it generates abundance for all those who share this space and this time.

If five hundred years ago our European brothers had developed an open cooperation with us and the land instead of striving to own us and the land, then the world would not be in the situation it is in today. The opportunity was missed at that time, and now it has returned. Elders and visionaries of more than one tribe are asking that their voices be heard, as well as the voices of Pachamama that speak through them. This is a calling to acknowledge the original wisdom that all humans have, as it is expressed by people of Indigenous cultures and of all ancient lineages still alive on Earth. Wisdom, generosity and compassion should be the main driving forces behind the world's economy, not the business plans of investors who can't see yet that it is impossible to make themselves truly happy without making everybody else happy.

All that is natural works, matching the original designs that are born from the Great Sacred Power's intelligence which keeps the entire universe organized between the forces of chaos and the ones of equilibrium. This power is constantly multiplying lives and giving opportunities for an infinite amount of beings, old and new. Tribal economy is rooted in the simple recognition of that which works in favor of living well and healthy, all together on this planet – "all" meaning not only all humans but all forms of life for whom this Earth and this time are their home.

In my humble opinion, creating natural and ecological products is not enough for changing the destructive ways of the modern economy. In truth, our whole economic system needs to become natural, ecological and sacred. This will be possible when the consequences of all that we do are measured, taking a serious look at their possible effect on the health and well-being of all people, all forms of life, and generations to come. As long as we perpetuate a system in which profit is number one on the list of priorities, very little can change. Would it be that bad for profit to be number two on the list? The first urgent necessity is that those who have economic and political power, no matter how large or small, regain their freedom to use the heart when making decisions that affect the lives of others.

I don't believe that Indigenous people are in need of a political victory or an ideological one. What we need is to know that all of us, the human race, have regained our direction – and what remains of the Amazon jungle may continue living and reproducing, dolphins and whales may continue inhabiting the ocean full of joy without illnesses caused by the contamination of the waters, polar bears do not lose the precious ice on which they walk, and jaguars do not lose their jungle trees and can continue drinking pure water from the rivers. We want all beings to feel relieved by knowing that we humans have returned to our place as caretakers of life, that we have agreed to stop the destruction, and that we will light our sacred fires to create refined vibrations for the nourishment of all beings.

THE TRIBAL WAY

What do our rituals and sacred fires have to do with the economy? Our awareness is activated by our ceremonies, because ceremonies open our heart and give us the chance to remember what is really important. We return to the sacred fire, to our prayers and celebrations in order to remember how much we love all that is alive and how much we want to live. To put it in the simplest way, we return to our ceremonial spaces in order to feel our heart. Then our motivation and inspiration to do our task as guardians of life is renewed. When we remember our true nature, we feel good and content for being what we are.

Tribal economy, the natural economy of the children of the Earth and the Sun, is born from our natural talents; it is our birthright. This economy requires the sharpening of our intelligence to become capable of balancing the forces of Nature that we affect with our actions. This economy also requires heart, so with generosity and reciprocity we continuously look for the well-being of all life.

The tribal way is based on the generous circulation of goods and a deep caring for the health of the natural sources of life. Therefore, it allows the human economy to be part of the most successful economy ever known: the universal economy. The amount of resources, energy, and blessings that circulate on Earth is so vast that no one could even imagine it. The Sun actually radiates 15,000 times more energy than what is needed in order to meet the demands of our entire planet. The Universe and the Earth are not poor. On the contrary, they are abundance itself. It is we humans who create poverty when we create wealth in an unbalanced, unwise fashion.

UNCONDITIONAL LOVE IS AN ECONOMIC ISSUE

In the old days, there was no money, and so the lack of money didn't make anybody poor. Now it is different. Economic power is based on money. A long time ago there was the practice of barter that allowed for the possibility of showing reciprocity from the heart. To be grateful and help those who help you was not a condition but something born from the heart. Paying a fee can easily leave the heart aside, as the payment is just about fulfilling an obligation. On the other hand, taking the time to choose something to give to another as an act of reciprocity and gratitude is always an action of the heart.

The way we generate our economy is strongly correlated to the spiritual quality of the world we are creating. Our economy can be generated from the heart, opening the possibility for a culture of the heart to be developed in the world.

Now that there is money and the custom of putting a price on goods and services, some Indigenous people feel forced to be extremely careful. It is very difficult to live in two different worlds at the same time; it makes us feel like we are suffering from multiple personalities – and it is easy to make mistakes. Which is the voice to follow when they are both so loud? One voice says to go with the ruling system and sell what you can, even your traditions and your spiritual gifts, so you can have more money.

Another voice says that some things are not for sale and keeping our integrity has no price.

The ways that we inherited from our Indigenous ancestors are becoming mixed with the rules of marketing. Now, we have to be very careful because the best that we have to share with the world is the way of the heart. We could lose ourselves if we embark on a competition for getting "clients." Our ancestors did not have clients; they had relatives whom they helped unconditionally, trusting that they understood the need for reciprocity. How do we deal with people who do not understand the refined ways of reciprocity? Do we become like them or patiently wait for them to learn? I personally believe that it is our task to give a good example of how strong our will can be when we decide that our love for the people and the Great Sacred Power is unconditional. We need to trust in that which we want others to trust: that the Great Sacred Power will always give us what we need.

Nowadays, people from different cultural and racial backgrounds are approaching our villages and our ceremonies, looking for healing and for a place to remember themselves. The permanent growth of the tourism industry in Peru, for example, is happening in part because of foreigners in search of a mystical experience. In truth, this is good news; however, it gives us a lot of responsibility as it brings us the temptation of using this situation to become less poor, and maybe rich.

I have witnessed so many times to what happens in Indigenous sacred ceremonies. When the Cosmic

Mother feels touched by a sacred fire lit by the humans, she responds with contentment and generosity. Magic happens after the fire is lit and the offerings and petitions have been made. She and her powerful creatures give us rain, good harvests, knowledge, wisdom, inspiration, vision, joy in the heart and healing power.

These gifts are emanations from her sacred womb, generously given to us humans so that through us they may continue their course. They are not meant to be captured by us and become our possessions. They are a gift from Her to us and not really our belongings. How can someone sell what is not theirs? They were given to us so they could go through us and continue on their way, nourishing all that is hungry and healing all that is sick. Therefore, it is delicate for an Indigenous healer, instructor, or ceremonial leader to put a monetary value on these spiritual gifts that are meant to be given to those who need them. These gifts are for the well-being of everybody and not for personal profit or personal greatness. Ceremonies and spiritual powers cannot be put up for sale because no one can be the owner of Spirit, which is love and freedom in its essence. The understanding of the Elders of more than one tribe is that if someone decides to put them up for sale, these spiritual goods would have to lose their essence of love and freedom and become *something else*. This *something else*, even when it may be useful, doesn't have the same power of the original gift given by Spirit.

Based on what I have been able to see with my own eyes, I believe that what today is called *shamanism* has some of the wisdom of the Indigenous peoples, but it also has a lot of the influence of marketing. With all my heart, I wish my brothers and sisters who work for Spirit, serving the people, never suffer from lack in their lives and always have what they need to provide for their families. I just want to share what Spirit has shown me many times: spiritual laws and the laws of marketing do not combine well. When they are combined, the consequence is a degeneration of the powerful rituals that our ancestors passed on to us.

The main requirement so that our rituals work and are preserved in their full integrity is that they be unconditional, with the heart commanding, full of generosity and compassion. When the service is unconditional, the Great Sacred Power shows up. This power is the source of the healing and blessings that the people receive. Then, it is up to the people to decide how they want to show reciprocity, both to the ones who perform the ritual and to the Sacred Powers. In the way of the Lakota people, as in many Indigenous tribes, those who receive favor from a ceremony later sponsor a gratitude ceremony to feed the spirits and the people who worked on their behalf. This they do from their heart, and what they give, large or small, is what they wish to give and not an obligation.

Loving without conditions is an economic issue. All of us, Indigenous and non-Indigenous, who have something to offer humanity so the heart comes back to economic practices should do it with full passion and enthusiasm, because it is something the world really needs. When human societies are truly walking a good path, their spiritual life and their economic system match. When they don't match, then something needs to be checked. Good prayers should be followed by good actions that truly serve the well-being of all life and not just our own or that of our family or of those who belong to our church or to our country. All the practices of unconditional reciprocity and generosity that have been mentioned are both economic and spiritual practices. They have the power to connect and blend our spiritual and material aspects, with our heart shining in the middle.

None of us want more wars. Because I do not want my children and all the other children to experience the atrocities of war in their lifetime, I insist on saying, with the loudest voice, that the unconditional love we so often speak about has to be reflected in the way we run our economy. We all need to be genuinely willing to do our *give away* and participate in the generous circulation of vital energy – or money if you want to see it that way – around the planet and for the well-being of all life. Far from being a romantic idea, this issue, from my point of view, is a matter of life or death for future generations.

6

PEOPLE SUFFERING
IN PARADISE

Loving without conditions is an economic issue, and
so is war.

As I shared in chapter two when speaking about
the ancient Caral nation, to receive confirmation
that war is not a necessary condition for the
development of a civilization was for me a great
relief. I wish that all the books that contain this false
statement be removed from the schools where our
children learn. Nowadays, thinking that civilizations
are founded in war justifies big budgets for military
infrastructure and makes even the presidents of
democratic nations serve as chiefs of the army. I
hope with all my heart that in the future the people
who run our countries don't need to be warlords.

I learned a great deal about war while in the
jungle of northern Colombia – a territory of
Indigenous tribes, of farmer communities, of
paramilitary and guerrilla armies, and of very
precious forms of wildlife. I have walked for endless
hours in the mud, surrounded by the beautiful green
hills of the high rainforest, smelling the aromas of

paradise, listening to the songs of the multicolored birds, and remembering our instructions: "Do not step out of the marked path. This whole place is mined."

My visit to Colombia happened thanks to an invitation from a group of European activists who organized a pilgrimage in solidarity with the people of a farming community. For years, this farming community had been dealing with the assassination and displacement of its members by either paramilitary or guerrilla forces – and, at times, even by the official police and army.

Father Javier, a very gentle and humble Jesuit priest, had supported the members of this farming community in their decision to become a Peace Community – a place where weapons are not allowed and with a clear public statement that they do not take sides with any of the parts of the armed conflict.

As is customary for Indigenous people before going into any important mission, we pray, asking for permission and for the good company and support of the sacred spirits of the Earth and the Sky. Without knowing how Father Javier would respond to my proposal, early in the morning on the day we were beginning our many-day pilgrimage through the jungle, I volunteered to run a traditional ceremony, an offering to the spirits of the mountains of that region. We needed the blessing of Pachamama as we were about to walk through a war zone. After receiving Father Javier's permission, respecting his position as the spiritual leader of the community, we went ahead and started our ceremony. Soon after, the moment came when I had to ask Father Javier if he wanted to contribute with his own prayers. And he prayed holding three coca leaves in his hands like Indigenous people do, and all of his words came directly from his heart. As I heard him pray, I realized who this man was and felt immensely grateful and honored to be praying with him. He encouraged the members of the community – mostly Christian farmers descendants of Indigenous people – to pray in these Indigenous ways, loving the Earth as one loves a mother. He told everyone how sad it was for him that such beautiful spiritual ways were getting lost in those mountains of Colombia.

I wasn't really expecting what happened next as we started walking on our pilgrimage. What the members of the Peace Community had in mind was not only to walk with us, but also to stop at every single place where someone had been killed or a massacre had occurred and tell us the story, right there on the spot where innocent people had spilled their blood. This went on and on for six long days. They really wanted us to know their stories so we could tell them to the rest of the world, and their stories left us broken inside, our hearts bleeding the same as theirs.

First I heard a story from a beautiful elder who lives in the village, a woman named Brigida. She showed us the picture of her fifteen-year-old daughter and expressed her pain for having lost her at such a young age. Her daughter went to dance with her friends one night, and afterwards went to sleep in a cabin with many other teenagers. She never saw the dawn of that day; paramilitary soldiers entered the cabin and shot them all in their sleep. The government offered her a certain amount of money as compensation for the death of her child, and looking straight into my eyes she asked, "How much is the life of my daughter worth?" She refused to receive this money, even when she, like everyone else in the village, has to live in the most humble conditions.

What is the cause of death for such young people? If they do not join the paramilitary army they are accused of being guerrilla; if they do not join the guerrilla, then they are accused of being with the paramilitary – an extra-official army created by the government to fight the guerrilla army without being bound by the laws of the country.

We were told by community leaders that they declared themselves *Comunidad de Paz de San Jose de Apartado*, or a Peace Community, in 1997 to avoid constantly having to decide between two or three bad choices. They wanted to be free to choose peace, as they knew very well that every time they took sides with one they became enemies and targets of the other. Seeing that their lives were torn apart by a war that they had not chosen, they decided to no longer take sides with violence. They officially declared themselves a peaceful pueblo in which firearms are not allowed, and its members refuse to carry them. I was there and clearly saw the large sign at the entrance of their village: "WE ARE A PEACE COMMUNITY. WEAPONS ARE NOT ALLOWED PAST THIS POINT. WE

DO NOT DRINK ALCOHOL. ALL OUR WORK IS COMMUNI-TARIAN."

After making this radical change in their community, things actually got worse for them. One hundred and eighty-seven members of the peace community have been murdered since 1997 – many of them by paramilitary forces, some of them by the military, and others by the guerrillas. Hundreds of families have been displaced from their villages, forced to leave their homes, fields, and animals. My interpretation of these painful events is that in getting out of the violence game, they became a threat for those who think that this game is necessary. I think it is possible that the potential to infect the entire Colombian population, provoking the creation of other peace communities in areas of violence, turned out to be unacceptable for those who benefit from the war.

Colombia is truly a paradise, full of natural wonders and very beautiful people. Sometimes paradise, for those like the people I got to know, becomes hell. Paradise becomes hell when someone wants to become the exclusive owner of Mother Earth's beauty, of her abundant and marvelous generosity, of the gold, the trees, the waters, and all kinds of delicious fruits. Children have to grow up with fear and trauma. Youngsters who can carry a weapon want to be hired and converted into killers – and may end up walking for the rest of their lives without their heart. Everybody you meet in the peace community has lost someone in the most horren-dous way. Their hearts and minds are permanently getting hit by acts of terror, and the official authorities and the media call them terrorists in order to justify their deaths.

Wars like the one in Colombia are always for ownership of land, for territorial disputes, for the resources that exist within the territory, or for some advantage that the territory offers. There is gold, there are large water reservoirs, there are some of the biggest banana plantations in the world, there are precious trees and medicinal plants, and there are "multinational development plans" for the area. Displacing the Indigenous people and the farmers so the land may be vacant, I believe, is the ultimate goal.

Once displaced from the so called "conflict zone," Indigenous people and farmers end up losing their homes, food sources, and ancient sacred places. Whether it is the northern Colombia of today or the sacred Black Hills of South Dakota one hundred years ago, the territories declared to be armed conflict zones always wind up being huge sources of natural resources or a strategic place for a new commercial venture. So in this case, like in many other wars, young people give their lives or lose their physical and mental integrity only to help unknown people gain territory needed for commercial enterprises.

Most times when I see battlefields, I cannot see the politics. I only see green trees, running waters, and little creatures. I only see Pachamama. All of these precious lands under dispute are originally Pachamama, Mother Earth, the mother of us all.

Like any other mother, she doesn't make distinctions when having to feed her children. She doesn't look at how much money you have in your pocket when allowing you to kneel down and drink pure water from a creek. The only condition for receiving her fruits, anywhere, is to be hungry. She is the provider of all things that make it possible for everybody, without exception, to continue living.

Almost at the end of our pilgrimage, we were walking back to what that day was our camp in a village called La Esperanza, and we stopped at the river to cleanse our bodies and souls. The last couple of days we had been followed by paramilitary soldiers. We saw them hiding behind trees or sometimes crossing the path right in front of us, with war paint on their faces, to let us know they were there. When we started our walk, we did it without knowing what could happen to us. We just had to do it. And now, after many days, we felt like something needed to be washed off our bodies, something sticky that the body accumulates when being so close to a bringer of death whose heart is absent.

In the river, I connected with two good brothers, and we laughed playing in the water like kids, enjoying the feeling of being alive. They were young men from the Nasa tribe of Colombia, who were participating in the pilgrimage. While we bathed in the river, we shared our awareness of being brothers and how much we had in common. We discovered that even though we came from different Indigenous nations, our way of understanding the world in which we live was the same, and the practices and ceremonies that brought us to this understanding were slightly different in form but in essence identical.

On that trip to Colombia, I had the honor of meeting a total of fifty members of the Indigenous guard created by the Nasa tribe. The members of this guard do not fight. With only their wooden staffs, they stand in front of any army that wants to violate the rights of the native people, willing to die defending what is just. While I was sharing time with them, they invited me to come to a peaceful demonstration that was going to happen the following week on October 12th, the anniversary of Christopher Columbus arriving on this continent. Unfortunately, it wasn't possible for me to stay longer in Colombia at that time, and I say unfortunately because when they told me the purpose of their non-violent mobilization in the streets, I really felt connected to it. They were going to request the liberation of Mother Earth. They didn't want to argue anymore with those who had taken away so much of their territory about the legitimate owners of the forests and mountains. They were now asking for Mother Earth to be freed, insisting that She belongs to Herself, and that we can all enjoy Her together. I love this way of seeing things!

Imagine what would happen if Mother Earth is freed from the possessive grasp of human greed and territorial competition. There wouldn't be more people putting mines under Her skin. She wouldn't get bombed, and She wouldn't have to weep when feeling the blood of innocent children penetrate Her body. This issue, apparently a political issue, is really a spiritual issue. Liberating Mother Earth we liberate ourselves from the tension we live in, always competing for territory and wounding ourselves on the way. We can just take care of Her, and let Her take care of us. With no doubt, She will give us all we need. When we pay attention, She is the one who teaches us that loving without conditions is truly an economic issue.

The idea of liberating Mother Earth can seem totally absurd for those who don't see the Earth as a being; however, for those guided by Indigenous mentality, it is a totally natural and reasonable idea. This is why Bolivia – a country with a majority of Indigenous people – following an initiative that actually started in Ecuador, has stated in its Constitution that Mother Earth has the same rights to life as a human being. This means that, legally speaking, there is the possibility of judging crimes against Mother Earth the same way crimes against human life are judged. And not only that, I heard that they decided that in their Constitution the term "natural resources" has to be replaced by the term "Earth Blessings."

A week later I was back home, and there was news about the protest of the Nasa tribe. Three members of the Indigenous guard, unarmed as usual, died when military soldiers opened fire on October 12, 2008 – the anniversary of Christopher Columbus' arrival. Their proposal to liberate Mother Earth turned out to be so threatening that they were killed for it.

The Indigenous Nasa nation, just like the rural Peace Community of San Jose de Apartado, is now going through what thousands of Indigenous nations around the world have had to go through for the past five hundred years. It is what happened to my Andean ancestors and then later to my Lakota relatives just one hundred and twenty years ago. The same thing is happening now to Indigenous people from remote areas of Central and South America, and to rural communities that aspire to become part of the modern world. Their lands are very valuable. Their wise way of life and self-sufficiency exempts them from having to be anyone's clients. But it seems that there are those people who would like all of us to be their clients, would like to see us go to the cities to become consumers in the markets and, among other things, start buying water in plastic bottles. Definitely, there are those who would like to see us leave the countryside, so they can extract all the juices from our Mother Earth with their powerful machines.

The extermination of tribes has been practiced throughout many centuries and is still being practiced. This is the extermination of true human beings who love the Earth with all their heart, descendants of people who over centuries developed the talent and wisdom to be guardians of the life of mountains, rivers and forests. When the guardians are eliminated, anyone can claim to be the new owner of the land and start taking the precious natural resources – better described as Earth blessings – that belong to all of us, the flesh and bones of the Earth to which we all belong.

After my trip to Colombia, I was back in New Mexico and went to a supermarket to buy food. I picked up a few bananas like I had done so many times before, and this time, I noticed that little sticker they put on the bananas and looked at it with full attention. They were Colombian bananas from a place I had visited. It wasn't possible for me to avoid feeling the suffering of the people who did not own those bananas that they grew on their land. I could not buy them. Walking through the supermarket, seeing the faces of the farmers I met in Colombia, I was only able to take a few things, feeling the weight of something really heavy on my chest. In that moment, I became fully aware of the price of my convenience. How unconscious I had been before in not connecting the abundance of packaged products offered by the supermarket with the pain of people who are my people. I do not want to forget the ones who are killed or displaced from their land so that someone may run a banana business or extract petroleum for the gasoline in my car.

7

MUNAY
THE WILL OF THE HEART

Our Indigenous ancestors learned that the most important of all spiritual powers is what today people know as compassion, and it was mainly because of this that I chose to follow in their footsteps. Those who have the capacity to forgive are able to clear their mind and see the truth: it is not what some "enemy" does to us that makes us fall; it is the way we react.

The path of developing true compassion is very difficult, because you cannot let yourself become a victim or hold anger. You must become responsible for the condition of your own life, no matter what others do to you. You are called to develop a strong will to reduce your self-importance and keep caring for all life, including those who have hurt you. And neither of these are moral obligations; they are just a possible path of freedom.

My adoptive father Basil Brave Heart, an Elder of the Lakota tribe of the North American plains, told me that the Lakota name for the spiritual quality of compassion is *Wauncila*. Hearing him speak one day at a Sun Dance ceremony about the importance of developing compassion, I was very happy to see that the Lakota and my Andean ancestors share the same values. In Runasimi, the language of my people in Peru, the word to name this spiritual power is *Munay*.

In the understanding of our ancestors, we humans can become greedy and selfish, and when this happens, these are the forces that drive our actions. We also can become afraid and angry, and then we feel entitled to live by winning battles against others. Our Indigenous cultures encourage us to seek the awakening of our *Munay*, so we may become good people instead of being destructive and harmful to others. This spiritual power, *Munay* (Runasimi) or *Wauncila* (Lakota) is the perfect complement of capacities like vision and other strengths that are born from undertaking consistent spiritual practices. We do not want to develop personal power just to become superior or to have a good image or to always be able to get what we want. We mainly want to do it for the sake of serving our people and our Mother Earth in a strong and beautiful way. We also cultivate *Munay* to enjoy the experience of perceiving with our heart the wonderful presence of Spirit, as much as possible, in all that we do.

The compassion of the heart is the balance of personal power; we do well when we have both. To carry any kind of powerful weapon in our hands or in our minds without having first awakened the sacred fire in our hearts makes us dangerous people.

The meaning of the word *Munay* is as vast as the universe. The best way to translate it, according to my understanding, is: "the will of the heart." In some cases it means "love;" in other cases it means "wanting;" in other contexts it means "power." In the end, all these meanings are valid and could be put together. *Munay*, in a broader sense, is "the immense power that lives in the human heart that allows us to act in favor of what we love and what we want." For those who want to put it in a simpler way, it works to just say "compassion" or to just say "will." Sometimes, it is good to understand the entire meaning that our ancestors put in a word, because, in this way, we understand what kind of people they were and how it is that they perceived their reality.

In the Andes, when we say "I love you," we say *"noka munani,"* with this last word, *"munani,"* being a derivative of the word *Munay*. What strikes me most about saying it in the Runasimi language is that it doesn't just mean "I love you." It really means: "I have the will and the power to love you" as well as "there is compassion in my heart for you." Even in this last case, when meaning compassion, it is not a passive form of compassion that just remains in one's heart as a good feeling towards another. In truth, *Munay* is an active energy that makes compassion come together with the willpower that makes us enact our love with *tukuy sonkoy* – or the whole heart – with courage and with a deep desire to serve another.

AWAKENING HAPPENS AFTER DOING THE WORK

We are all born with the same tools and the same potential. Capacities like *Munay* are latent in each person, waiting to be fully awakened. These spiritual capacities are not something that we take for granted or that we claim to possess; we know that we need to always work on ourselves in order to develop them. All the teachings and the example of our Elders, as well as very intense ceremonies like Vision Quests and our sacred dances, lead us to awaken the sacred fire in our heart.

For the Lakota and for many other tribes, it is necessary to go on *Hanblecheyapi* (Lakota), the ceremony of crying for a vision. The time of being alone on the hill, praying while fasting during very hot days and very cold nights, is the sacred time in which we have our encounter with the Great Mystery. At this difficult time, we are in need of so much help that we sometimes ask for it crying like a child. Finding ourselves in a life or death situation, we are also driven to awaken our own will in order to help ourselves, and usually, when we start helping ourselves, a power much greater than us comes to our aid.

We seek an experience that allows us to recognize, from the depths of our flesh to the heights of our divine self, that the stronger powers of life come from Spirit, from the mind of Spirit, from the heart where Spirit dwells. When we feel like we are dying and suddenly witness the help that shows up for us, we recognize that *Unci Maka* (Lakota) or *Pachamama* (Runasimi), the Earth where we are sitting, is really our mother. We recognize that She has a very big *Munay* acting on our behalf. To be struck by Her *Munay* is like being struck by lightning. So much love! It is in this way that many of us feel for the first time our own *Munay* being born in our chest; it's like having the love of our Mother Earth help us with a "jumpstart." Then, it is up to us to keep that fire lit in our heart alive in our daily life.

During Vision Quest, help comes to some people from our Mother Earth; for others, it comes from Her as well as from the Sky or from the Mystery itself. We feel very fortunate when, while feeling like a tiny insect that is dying from thirst in the middle of nowhere, something so powerful and divine gives its attention to us. It could come in the shape of an eagle or just as a blue light or however the Great Mystery decides to show itself to us. We feel so good afterwards that suddenly "nowhere" becomes home, and all the wild creatures that surround us are friends and relatives. It is totally incomprehensible at that moment, but this is clearly what happens. Because of the immense gratitude we feel, we have no other choice but to fall on our knees and cry.

Those who have gone to the hill to cry for a vision have returned with a gift. It is a great gift to receive a vision of oneself, to increase the understanding of who one is and of what it is to be a real human being – part human, part spirit. It is a great gift to experience, directly and not from a book, the *Munay* of the Earth, the *Munay* of the entire universe, and the awakening of our own *Munay*. It feels so good to be alive!

Can you imagine a society where everyone has *Munay* in their heart, a world in which humans are not only loving people but people whose love and will to support what they love are one and the same thing? How would a society be where most people have gone to the hill and returned with a gift from Spirit? There are people, and among them several Indigenous tribes, still striving to preserve these ancient ways that lead to having vision and the will of the heart awakened. This is happening at the same time that mainstream society walks in the opposite direction.

I have met hundreds of beautiful people who I know would like to contribute to the healing of this world – even if their contribution is to work on their personal healing – but they cannot take any consistent action yet. My understanding is that their personal spiritual power is still waiting to be born or still so young that they don't know what to do or how to do it.

To have a life with *Munay*, with the will of the heart awakened and active, is to have a creative life that naturally serves the well-being of all. People who have activated the *Munay* in their heart are good medicine for everyone – not just because of their good intentions but also because their natural and real spiritual power is available to serve. Their presence alone may remove an obstacle, put light on the path, heal the ill, nourish the source of our nourishment, and help to make good dreams come true.

In times like the one we are living in now, when the continuity of life depends on us to make strong changes in the way we live and run our economy, many are feeling called to awaken their *Munay*. As we will see in the next chapter, when we move too slowly, sometimes the sacred powers come to help us.

8

THE MEDICINE
OF THE BLACK JAGUAR

I went to Colombia a second time, invited by the
same group of European friends. This trip was
during the big assembly of all the members of the
Peace Community referred to earlier in Chapter 6.
The gathering took place at a remote village of
farmers called Mulatos, which had once been
bombed. Because of the history of violence in this
area and because many community leaders in the
gathering had a price on their heads, I decided the
best offering that I could make was to find a place
where I could pray all the time. While everyone was
having meetings and working in the village, I went to
the river every day, from dawn until dark, with my
rattle and sacred tobacco for making offerings and
prayers.

Even when I did have food and water during
those days, the whole experience had the feeling of a
Vision Quest. I prayed with all my heart for the land
and for the people, and in doing so, in a very intense
way developed a strong connection with the spirit of

that particular jungle – as strong and deep as the connection that grows with another person. I could feel my words and songs penetrating the roots of the trees and entering deeply into the heart of the land, and I felt welcomed and encouraged to continue. I offered my wishes for the good health of all the people and all forms of life living in that forest. And as I was always tapping into the sacred fabric of that land, I was also touched by horrendous memories and present sorrows.

I spent four days doing this work, always in the same spot. On the fifth day, I took a long walk in the jungle, following the river and leaving the village and the people far behind me. Later that day, around sunset, I was getting ready to turn around and walk back to camp when a very impressive tree made me stop. The fallen tree was so tall that it went from one side of the river to the other. Its diagonal figure cut the horizon; its top never touched the ground, clinging to the tops of trees on the opposite side of the river. From where I was, it looked like a pathway to heaven. "The perfect path for a jaguar to climb from the river's shore to the top of the tree line," I said out loud, surrounded only by birds.

Now that the sun was shining in the horizon as it began to set, I had to stop and ask myself if I should continue going forward towards the impressive fallen tree or start going back to camp. A strong impulse from within made me continue walking forward, and my body must have known what was about to happen because my heartbeat suddenly got faster. When I arrived on the other side of the river at the place of the fallen tree, a black jaguar was standing there very still. Between us was only a stream about thirty feet wide with very shallow water running slowly over pebbles.

At sunset, the jungle is at the peak of her beauty. The green gets darker, and deep caves made of leaves begin to appear everywhere, housing the mysteries that are about to come. Whatever can still shine does so with much enthusiasm, reflecting the last sun rays. The water vibrating in the river and the black fur of the jaguar were the lights of the moment. Usually at this hour, birds sing louder to exchange words with all the creatures that wake up at night, making the most fascinating sounds. But this evening was different. The black jaguar was facing a man.

Growing up in Peru, many times I heard the stories of the *yanapuma* or the *yanaotorongo* – the black puma or the black jaguar. These stories were always fantastic and spooky, made up by people who found the bones of those attacked by the wild cat. Of course, there weren't that many stories told by people who actually saw a black jaguar in the jungle. Knowing this, I felt immediately at peace, ready to accept that my time to leave this world had most probably arrived. Even when the jaguar moved away from me and disappeared into the brush, I kept making myself ready. I still had at least an hour's walk back to the camp, and it was getting dark. Jaguars are excellent hunters. If she wanted me, she was going to get me, most probably from behind when I least expected it. Walking slowly, alert, and stopping often to check my surroundings, I headed for the camp. Despite the danger facing me, I was surprised to stay so calm. The presence of the jaguar had ignited my deepest senses and made me feel more alive than ever. In my prayer, I was clear: "Please don't take me today. I want to live for my daughters and to continue doing my work." When I finally arrived to the safety of the camp, I turned towards the dark jungle and gave thanks for my life, putting some tobacco in the river as an offering of immense gratitude to the powerful spirit of the black jaguar.

A few years before encountering the black jaguar face to face, she came to visit me in my dreams. I found myself cornered in my bedroom when she came in the middle of the night. Full of fear, I tried to wake up from the dream but couldn't. The dream ended only after seeing my own body covered with a layer of black fur, and the skin under the fur was very sick. A day after having this dream, an excruciating pain in my neck literally paralyzed me and kept me in bed for two weeks. I spent long nights awake, trying to avoid moving my head as doing this caused a pain that felt like lightning bolts striking inside my body. My time to change had arrived. Looking at the dark ceiling of my bedroom for endless hours, I could clearly recognize old unhealthy patterns that I carried in my mind and behavior that now had to die, one way or another. I had been too slow at making the necessary changes in myself, procrastinating, making excuses, thinking that tomorrow I would have more time than today to give attention to my wounds, my resentments, my ego, my fears, and all the bad habits that came from them.

Although my neck pain got better, things in my life didn't. Soon after, I lost my house, I lost my car, and I lost the woman I loved.

My life became so simple after losing so much that I felt immensely relieved. The sacred black light of the west, present in my dream in the shape of a black jaguar, showed up to help me finish what I could not finish by myself. I became free and was able to put my energy entirely into my spiritual commitment at a time when much work is demanded from those who are still hopeful for the healing and change of this world.

By the time I was walking in the jungle of Colombia, I was able to understand more deeply about the black jaguar's medicine. For Indigenous people of South America, the black jaguar is a much-respected spirit, related to death, to the healing powers of thunder and lightning, and to all sacred forces that purify and renew life when it becomes stagnant or sick. Its medicine provokes a fast healing that doesn't wait for a process to happen. It just shows up and says "enough of this" and terminates it. It doesn't act out of cruelty or to punish; this is a medicine that works to support life's balance. Even when it apparently brings death or destruction, in reality, it is protecting the health and continuity of life. Unlike other sacred powers, this one doesn't give us exactly what we ask in our prayers; it gives us what we really need, even when it hurts. When a power like the black jaguar shows up, it is time to change, and there is no possible negotiation.

In Colombia, the fact that I met the black jaguar after my four days of prayer made me see this experience as a gift from Spirit, a sacred gift that had something to do with the intention of my prayers. Feeling peaceful and without thinking, I got the message. Since that day, I have full certainty in my heart that all the abuse that causes so much pain and destruction in that beautiful jungle, as in so many other jungles and forests, is soon going to come to an end. I really couldn't say how, but I can see that the moment of change has surely arrived.

The morning after I survived our encounter, I had to go back to the black jaguar and bring her an offering to express my gratitude. So I got up early and returned to where I saw her, taking my prayer instruments with me as well as my friend Vera so we could pray together.

I found the spot where the jaguar had been when we met, thanks to clear markings that she had left on the ground. It was a precious, enchanted place right next to the river, with one big boulder all covered with green moss on one side and a few smaller rocks around it forming a natural circle. Tree branches hung over the place, making it somewhat dark even in the morning. In the center, between two round rocks, there was a little pond full of water. Picking up a few dry leaves floating on the surface of the water as I tried to clean it, to my surprise, I realized that it was a spring. The water looked black but was very clean, with two little fish dancing inside of it, circling all around. Vera and I offered tobacco to the place, presenting ourselves and asking for permission to pray. The vibration was very high and sacred. This was clearly a power place, a gift for anyone who has the blessing of finding it. We offered more tobacco – this time to the black jaguar – giving her thanks for showing us this place. The purpose became clear to us: we were being asked to pray to the spirit of the black water, the sacred water of Mother Earth's womb.

A Very Unusual Group of Singers

In our prayers, Vera and I asked for the liberation of Pachamama, our Mother Earth, from all those who exploit her without taking care of her. Not too far from where we were, paramilitary forces were finding excuses to displace innocent farmers from their homes in areas where multinational mining companies had found huge amounts of gold. We got news of several villagers from a place called Cordoba getting killed during the days we were there. We prayed for protection for the people. We prayed for the end of the wars that hurt the jungle, the animals, and the villagers. We asked that no actions based on greed have power over the land anymore and that a new and healthy reality be born from the holy water of the sacred womb of Mother Earth that lay before us. We prayed that the deep waters of Pachamama's womb be free from the contamination created by the mistakes that we humans made in the past, that it be healthy and strong again, that it be capable of giving birth and nourishing many generations to come – not only of humans but of all the forms of life that live on this Earth.

It is sad to see human actions that are harmful to life, unjust and rooted in corruption, grow freely year after year. As long as the pain is caused to "others," only a few make a stand to protect them. I feel relieved when someone who carries sacred power and is connected to the heart of life says: "Enough of this!" I have been screaming these words within myself for a long time. The sacred warrior, a beautiful black jaguar, must have known that, and she was so kind to me. Instead of jumping on my back and ending my life, she showed me a magic place with a source of the purest sacred water. In this place, I was able to pour the deepest prayer I carry in my heart.

Before leaving, I felt called to pick up my rattle and play it for a little while, waiting for a healing song to arrive in my heart. When I started singing it, right away, a little gray frog stood on a rock in front of the spring and joined in, singing loudly, clearly, and in harmony with my voice, perfectly matching the rattle's rhythm. Then a bird arrived and, standing on a branch of a nearby tree, she also joined in, singing in perfect counter-rhythm, elevating the song to a very intense and playful vibration!

Not even in dreams had this ever happened to me. I felt so content while singing with a frog and a bird. I felt so grateful for having been invited to participate in this prayer. The three of us together spontaneously created the most joyful vibration, helping to relieve the forest from decades of suffering.

9

THE TIME
OF THE BLACK JAGUAR

How many times in the previous centuries has the end of the world arrived for hundreds of Indigenous nations? How many times have our ancestors had to rebirth from the ashes of their destroyed worlds? Those were difficult moments when we learned to pray and to ask for help so that our people might continue living. In such painful situations, we rediscovered the power of our ceremonies and their capacity to connect us to the source of our well-being, peace, understanding and health. No matter how difficult times were for the survivors of a wave of destruction, they always had the opportunity to get their happiness back; they used the power of ceremony, their connection with Spirit, and the simple truth of the heart.

Indigenous peoples, as well as others around the world who saw their homes fall to the ground, know how important it is to ask for help from the sacred powers and how precious it is to know that we are truly being heard. This is why it is so important in our spiritual work that we keep the channels for our connection with Spirit impeccable. We are doing this right now. At this time, we are praying for Pachamama's healing as well as for our relatives of the wilderness and of the oceans so that they do not lose their homes and their sources of nourishment. We are preparing for what is coming and praying for humanity so that we may wake up and correct our course before it is too late. We are dancing and singing strongly and sending a voice to the universe saying that we want to continue living.

TIME TO CHANGE

It is time to change, and if we do not change something stronger than us is going to do it for us. We know this from experience. We know this because for thousands of years we have been observing the life-cycles of Pachamama. In Indigenous cultures and all ancient cultures of the Earth, there is the practice of studying the changes of the major cycles of life. This knowledge is important because cycles always have a beginning and an end that intensely affect our lives and our destiny.

Our ancestors observed the sun, the moon and the stars, and watched their cycles and their duration. They had the wisdom to live according to the nature of their time, like someone who dances to the rhythm of music being played. Thousands of years of experience have shown us that if we do not listen to the cosmic rhythm, we trip and fall.

Therefore, based on the wisdom of the ancestral nations, there exists the practice of getting ready to fully receive the blessings of certain cosmic dates – and to also get ready for the arrival of difficult times.

Times like the one we are in now are especially difficult. We are at the end of a long cycle where social and planetary change is born from a cosmic command that we humans have no other choice but to obey. These difficult times are good for us because of how they squeeze and change us. They contain the most valuable opportunities, and they could be dangerous for those who remain asleep and fail to develop a partnership with what has come to change us.

Sages of many Indigenous nations and other ancestral nations of the world say that we are now at the end of a very long cycle: the complete cycle of our present humanity. The Elders also say that the lack of preparation for the change that is coming is alarming.

There are small cycles, like the 500 year cycles; there are bigger cycles that last around 2,000 years; and there are even longer cycles, always containing smaller cycles within them. These longer cycles are the time of a complete *humanity* that lasts almost 26,000 years. According to the memory kept by some Indigenous nations, there were three other *humanities* before ours, so we are part of the *fourth humanity*. Now we are not only at the end of one long cycle of around 26,000 years, but we are also at the end of four of these cycles that amounts to 104,000 years of human experience. Many endings are happening at the same time, which means that a big change is ready to happen. These 104,000 years are the longest cycle we have ever completed. After this, the *fifth humanity* will begin.

I was very young when I had the fortune of receiving a beautiful teaching from my Elders in Peru, which helped me to understand the cycles of life. They explained that the complete cycle of a *humanity* goes through three movements or "times." First comes the time of creation, next comes the time of conservation, and last is the time of renewal. The time of creation is that magic time that today is talked about in myths, legends and stories. This is the time where the creative capacity of the humans, supported by strong cosmic forces, does not know the impossible. This is the time of designing and building the forms that will become vehicles and containers for the essences that want to be developed according to dreams and purposes that will manifest over thousands of years. This is a time of great power and happiness; the time of a true earthly paradise in which perfect temples and happy tribes of impeccable wisdom are born. It is also a time to receive instructions for taking the steps towards a certain spiritual and human growth. All of this is driven by an immense possibility of expanding consciousness to places never before visited by the human heart and mind. This is a time in which divine beings guide men and women.

After having enjoyed this time of creation for a few thousands years, the time of conservation arrives.

The creative forces begin to diminish, and now darkness is needed in order to temper what was created. In this time, humans are tested and learn how to become stronger by dealing with difficulties. Staying connected to the original creative forces requires effort or an infinite gracefulness. Some people go through this time in a good way – always singing, dancing and laughing – while others have a really hard time dealing with their suffering. Afraid of losing the light of the beginning, some of the humans in this time tend to become more conservative than creative, more educated than spontaneous. Others become rigid and authoritarian, creating rules and keeping traditions that are jealously passed from generation to generation.

Of the three times, the time of conservation is the longest. It always ends when the essence of the beginning has been forgotten, when magic can only be found in certain stories, and young people rebel against formalities that have no freshness or explanation. At the end of the time of conservation, there is also evident corruption by those who have held positions of power for a long time, leading to an epidemic loss of human values. The tension continues to grow until humanity becomes like a bomb ready to explode or a woman ready to give birth. Now the third movement arrives: the time of renewal. This is the shortest and most intense of the three, the time when purification is needed so life may continue.

UNDERSTANDING THE NATURE OF OUR TIME

Evidently, today we find ourselves living in the most intense time, the time of renewal. This is the time of a purifying chaos in which lies are seen for what they are, and there is a collective craving for returning to the simplest truth. At this confusing time, old group and ethnic identities become debilitated, and millions of humans lack clarity about their future and their true place in the world. The social pillars and belief systems of the conservative past are broken, and the new pillars are not built yet. There has been a great deal of learning during the struggles of the conservative time, but the time to harvest has not arrived yet. The collective state – which is similar to being in labor – contains pain, fear, and great hopes all mixed up. This time is the most difficult, and it also offers the most opportunities for those who seek their liberation from old mental prisons. This time is somehow dangerous for those who resist, because its energy is fierce and incontestable. It also has the potential to quickly bring back to the light all those who move their will in favor of real changes. Now is when the big change happens, so that a new time of creation may arrive and find hearts that are clean and open to see and support the unfolding of a new world, still unknown.

In times of renewal, it is the Black Jaguar who rules. At this time, it is common for many people to experience major losses in their lives; some are brutally taken out of their comfort zone. Many see their old life not working anymore or feel afraid when seeing destruction happen in the rest of the world. It all means just one thing: it is time to change.

WHAT MAKES CHANGE POSSIBLE

I am of the opinion that while talking about change is good, it does not create change. According to what I have seen, real change happens in three different ways. The first way is a gift from Spirit, an enormous blessing that comes to us unexpectedly through a dream, some extraordinary encounter with a being, or an event that awakens our mind. I consider this kind of gift to be like a "loan" from Spirit so that we have the necessary spiritual "capital" to start doing our own work. The second way is the way of the black jaguar, which comes and says "Enough!" and destroys the prisons where we feel safe and comfortable so we wake up. The third way is what in the Andes we call *Munay*, the will of the heart. This path of the heart's will makes us persevere in the development of new habits and constantly seek encounters with the sacred sources that support our awakening. In times of renewal, like the one we are in now, I see that change happens for people from any of these three sources; however, given that we are running out of time, the prevalent way is the fastest: the one of the black jaguar. And even when I believe this to be true, I was instructed to always keep choosing the path of my heart's will.

To be waiting for blessings to come and change me – or for an attack of the black jaguar to come and "kill" me, my ego, and all my bad habits – leaves me like a leaf at the mercy of the wind; it makes my life swing from blissfulness to pain, over and over again. But the swings are less frequent if I develop my own will. Instead of being at the mercy of the forces that come to wake me up, I prefer to choose to wake up and do my own work. Doing so will not stop the forces that bless or shake us; but I have experienced many times how different it is when these forces arrive and my will is in its place. Instead of feeling totally dependent on what they do to me, I have the opportunity to do my best to dance with them, to feel a partnership and collaboration with them. I feel this is similar to the difference between being a baby and being an adult. When we are babies, we totally depend on our parents to stay alive; when we are adults, we may still have our parents and receive their help and guidance, but in a very different way because now we are responsible for the condition of our own lives.

10

THE CHANGE OF PERCEPTION

The first time I was a witness to the change of the world was also the first time I experienced a total change of my perception. I had not enough will yet, so I received a gift from heaven – an enormous blessing that activated my desire to always be close to Spirit, a desire that has never left me since then. I was twenty years old when this happened. Walking in the streets of Ollantaytambo, a town that our ancestors built in what is now called the Sacred Valley of the Incas in Peru, I had an unexpected encounter with an Indigenous man. That night he invited me and a group of friends to his house where we listened with great attention to the stories he had to tell us. Feeling captivated by this man's knowledge about the way of life of our remote ancestors, my heart opened up to the ancestral memory to the extent that, little by little, my mind entered an altered state of consciousness.

Suddenly, everything was clear in my mind. All the stories that I heard from this man stopped being new knowledge. I always knew what he was going to say before he said it, as if my own memories were awakening and coming out of his mouth.

At some point during the night, I needed to release my bladder, so I went outside to find a tree. As I stepped out, I was surprised by the ocean of stars that I saw over my head. In the Andes, we know many constellations, especially the ones near the Southern Cross, and one of them is called the Eyes of the Llama: two stars next to each other like two little eyes looking at us from the sky. Just a moment after stepping out of the house, I found myself looking precisely at these two stars. I was looking at them so intensely that it felt as if each one of my eyes got hooked to one of the stars. Indeed, I was hooked. I tried to move my body, and I couldn't. I wanted to lower my head to free myself from this strange sensation, but it was impossible. In that moment, I clearly heard someone right behind me playing a very beautiful melody on a *quena*, an Andean flute, and I had the most shocking realization that the music being played was the exact expression of the feelings happening inside of me. At first, I enjoyed the melody so much that I surrendered to the experience of being hooked to the stars and relaxed with total abandon; but, after a while, I felt deeply tired and began to feel scared. Deciding that it was enough, I tried again to move my body. But I was still para-lyzed. The melody being played by someone behind me became much more intense at that moment, and I felt my spirit being elevated to unknown levels, arriving at a state of ecstasy as if I was ready to explode. Meanwhile, the sensation in my eyes was one of receiving a steady charge of energy that was coming from the two stars. For the second time, I surrendered to the experience, accepting, smiling as I became aware of my own laziness and lack of will, giving thanks for having been forced to go further, overcoming my limitations – the ones that were in my mind.

Once everything in me was smiling and I had stopped resisting, the music regained its initial softness and cradled me with immense tenderness. A bit later, the music stopped and at the same instant my head became abruptly unhooked from the stars. I turned around and there was no one behind me. The biggest surprise came a minute later. When I went back to the house, my friends were still singing the same song that they had been singing when I had left. I was sure that my experience had lasted something like half an hour, but it had been only a couple of minutes. Without saying a word, I stayed a little longer with my friends and then went to sleep.

The next day was the first day of a new life, and I no longer was the same person that I had been before. Neither was the world the same world in which I had lived before. It seemed to be that my eyes had been washed by the blue light of the stars, and this made me see things in a different way. Everything was permeated by a brighter light, and I felt happy to be alive. I found beauty in all things that I had never found before. My capacity to feel compassion for people was much greater. It was a new experience for me to realize how strong my capacity was to comprehend what people were going through in their lives. I could accept any kind of behavior from people without any judgmental reaction. On this day, the world changed into a more peaceful world. What created this change was a change in my perception. Since that day, I am aware that the change of the world somehow happens inside of me first – after my perception has changed.

According to what I have learned, there are three ways in which change can happen: thanks to a blissful experience like the one I had with the stars called The Eyes of the Llama, thanks to the unquestionable intervention of the power of the "black jaguar," or thanks to actions born from our own will. Sometimes too, there is a combination of events where two or all the ways just mentioned come together. In the end, regardless of where it was motivated from, change has the potential to be real and consistent when there has been a profound change in our perception of the reality in which we live.

Always choosing the path of will, I see change as the sacred experience of moving my perception to the "other side. " At the other side, the reality is different, luminous and healthy, and I am only able to go there when riding on the *perpetual sacred motion.*

To change the reality is the ultimate healing. Therefore, I often find myself activating my spiritual awareness, so that I can recognize the presence of the perpetual sacred motion when it is in front of me. It may appear as the wind or the smile of a child or the unexpected visit of a bird. When it becomes difficult to perceive the presence of something sacred in ordinary reality, I choose to climb a mountain or go to a ceremony or do unconditional service – situations in which the motions of the sacred can be more easily met.

THE POWER OF SACRED TIME

I believe that we all were born with the ability to change our perception; therefore we all can change the world. This change of perception is a very profound experience when it happens in sacred time.

When the time of our ordinary mind stops, we enter into the time of Spirit, the sacred time, the time when everything is possible. My first experience in which I became aware of the existence of sacred time was a gift that came to me from the stars. Since then, I have made sure to have the will to look for this type of experience over and over again when participating in Indigenous ceremonies.

Every time we leave the space where a ceremony has just taken place, I feel surprised when seeing that the world outside is different; that it has changed. Somehow it looks more luminous and beautiful as a whole and in every single detail. What is it then that changes the world? In my experience, the world changes when our perception changes from the inside because we have made an inner movement that allowed us to perceive from a different place. And this other world, a better world, only comes to existence when we are capable of perceiving it.

I agree with those who say that it is more about remembering than about changing; it is about returning to a place that was always there, but we had forgotten. This change of our perception that brings us back home is caused by a super intense experience where we have liberated ourselves from our conditioned human mind and entered the abundant and magic time of Spirit.

Some of the most beautiful moments of my life were when I shared the experience of being in ceremony with my family and my community. Indigenous ceremonies are always sacred and full of the beauty of the songs and all the sacred instruments that we use to work on elevating our vibrations to a high spiritual level. But they are not always easy. On many occasions, the peak of the ceremony is reached only after we have dealt with our shadow side and faced some truths that we had been blind to before the ceremony. After this, all is so good. I enjoy so much seeing the faces of my people washed by Spirit, feeling their awakened heart as they pray, realizing that we all together have remembered our original nature. There, in that healthy place and in that sacred time to which we all arrive together, everybody is talented, everyone is beautiful. When our voices come together, we recognize what a capacity we have to sing, to vibrate together in the most elevated place. In a simple and natural way, something flows out of our beings like humming-birds coming out of our mouths, and exquisite warmth radiates out from our hearts. These vibrations are offered to all our relations and to the well-being of all life; they nourish and make more beautiful the sources of our life and everything that needs this sacred food in order to continue living.

THE END OF TIME

Thanks to the ceremonies inherited from our ancestors of the Andean mountains and Amazon jungles, and thanks also to the generous sharing of the Lakota people of North America whose ceremonies are now an important part of my life, I have been able to continue developing a constant relationship with sacred time.

Twenty-five years after my experience with the two stars in Ollantaytambo, I had another experience in which time as we normally know it ceased to exist. This happened one night when I was conducting a medicine ceremony for a young girl who needed a cure for her illness. On that occasion, we had used the help of a sacred plant from South America to travel to the spirit world and find the help that she needed. The ceremony was very intense and beautiful, and at the end I felt content seeing that we had been blessed with a generous amount of help.

After the ceremony, I went to change my clothes, but before leaving I asked the young girl and the other participants to stay close to the fire a bit longer as the spirit of the medicine and its effects were still with us. I was putting on my pants when I felt something extremely heavy in one of the pockets. I reached inside and found a watch. Then I did what in so many years of doing ceremonies I had never done: I looked at the time. I still remember that the watch said it was 1:05 a.m.

I went to the fire and, to my surprise, the ceremony was not over. The medicine was still acting on us so strongly that we had a beautiful and intense experience, all together, speaking truth, liberating our souls in front of the fire. I felt this lasted at least one or two hours and then, feeling released by the power of the medicine, I said good night and started walking to where I was going to rest.

As I was walking, again I felt an uncomfortable weight in one of my pants pockets and immediately went for the watch, as if driven by an outer force. When I saw the time, I froze on the spot. It was still 1:05 a.m., and the watch was running and working well. Time had stopped. While we had continued having an entire sequence of experiences, the watch was not able to register the passage of the time we were in together. Becoming aware that this had just happened put me again in an altered state of consciousness, and the power of the medicine came back to me.

I was finished assisting the young girl, so the spirit of the medicine decided it was my turn to receive help. The power of the medicine stayed with me all night. There was an old woman in my vision, speaking to me and showing me intense pictures related to some healing I had to do for myself. As at the fire, the experience was highly intelligent and wise, rooted in a limitless, total freedom for my heart to be open to the truth and to the divine compassion that brings this truth to us. Every once in a while, the old woman interrupted my journey to ask me to look at my watch again. Every time, I played at guessing: "I am sure that now twenty minutes have passed." I looked at the watch and only two minutes had passed. So this was a very long night, with lots of learning.

I must have had this kind of experience hundreds of times in previous years. I just was not as aware of it as when being pushed by the old woman to notice the difference between the two times – the inner sacred time and the one of the watch.

This reflection leads me to the Mayan Calendar, which, contrary to what many people have been made to believe, does not speak about the end of the world. It speaks about the end of time. What does it really mean that the calendar ends? It is not the end of life. It is only the end of time as in the case of my spiritual journey when my watch wasn't able to record the movement of my inner reality. All healers seek for this experience of no time because there is nothing more powerful for creating change and healing. My understanding is when the Mayan Elders speak about the end of the calendar, they are referring to a cosmic experience in which the sacred forces of the universe will act as the catalyst of change and healing through the experience of *no time*.

It is the cosmic reset button being pressed. When time ends, the effects of all that comes from the past are neutralized for the new beginning to be pure, free, uncontaminated. This event, the end of the movement of time, is more profound than a physical event; it is a spiritual experience that has an immense potential to change our perception of our world. It has to do with the state of our being. It is a cosmic spiritual event offering the opportunity of change to all humanity. We know a little of how this works because of our participation in healing ceremonies. The ultimate healing is always the total renewal of life, the offering that *Taku Wakan Skan Skan*, that "Something Sacred in Perpetual Motion," gives us to have a clean new start, so we can leave the mistakes and pains of the past behind us.

The reward for our efforts comes when time is over – when the future is no longer a consequence of our past but a new reality, born from the Cosmic Mother who became pregnant with our prayers, dreams and visions.

11

THE TEACHINGS
OF THE SPIDER

A long time ago, I had my own cravings to return to the simple truth. I wanted to know what I had to change in myself. So I decided to take the opportunity of changing my perception, making use of the tools that have worked for Indigenous people since ancient times. I took the path of Vision Quest, a path that leads to the experience of sacred time and spiritual intensity.

Knowing that the sacred power that renews all life – the time of the black jaguar – may arrive at any moment to wake us up in painful ways, we consciously choose to go through ceremonies of life renewal. During Vision Quest we endure many days without food and water while praying on the hill. In these ceremonies, Indigenous people intentionally get close to death; not from wanting to physically harm ourselves but to liberate the flow of our lives from certain heavy energies that create stagnation, illness and oblivion.

THE GIFT OF SPIRITUAL VISION

This may be hard to believe for those who are not familiar with the Vision Quest ceremony, but it really happened to me that I had a full conversation with a spider who became my teacher at the moment of our encounter. Why did a little spider take it upon herself to help me see something really important? Who sent her? What was the source that started her movement towards the center of my awareness? When asking these questions, I don't need an answer. All I feel is an ocean of gratitude and happiness, knowing without a doubt that a higher spiritual power is always watching over us and that this sacred power is not far away in heaven, but everywhere we are.

Wakan Tanka, the Great Sacred Creative Power, gives us visions and dreams. When we are able to sustain these visions and dreams, we end up impregnating the Cosmic Mother with them, and later we see a new reality being born around us and within us.

We too are spirits. Creators take care of their creatures. Because we are one with it, the Great Spirit provides us with visions and dreams that we can then use to contribute to the healthy continuity of all life.

In the Great Circle of Life, everything is connected as well as cared for by a divine power. During Vision Quest, we receive the blessing of realizing that we are inside of this great circle, and recognize that, as part of it, we are always being taken of by something very sacred. When we don't feel taken care of, it is just because we are not available to the source – caught in our heads, too busy, distracted, or with our doors closed.

Vision Quest is the ceremony of becoming available to Spirit. One of the ways to describe what we experience as "Spirit" is an immense sacred power in permanent motion. This sacred power circulates around the Universe, touching all forms of life on its way, like an immense cosmic musician playing his instruments.

The third time I went on a *Hanblecheya* cere-mony, also known as a Vision Quest, the medicine man – my older brother and Elder – took me to a place on the hill where there was a very tall pine tree in the middle of a large open area. The trunk of this tree was thin and its top was very high, so I didn't get any shade during my days of fast and was blasted by the sun's heat. All the same, I was very grateful for being able to count on the company of this tree during my days on the hill.

Soon after I was left alone, I discovered why this was the best place for me to be left to fast and pray for many days and nights: the tree was partially burned in the bottom, and the scar left by the fire made a little cove where there were hundreds of spiders. "Hello relatives," I said respectfully and then prayed on my knees, asking them for permission to stay at their house for a few days. Even though they walked on top of my body pretty often, I never got a single bite.

It was one of those spiders that gave me a powerful vision. She was a very handsome, little light green spider. At first, I saw her standing on one of my naked toes. Then she started walking up my leg, taking a long time to walk over me and reach her destination in the center of my chest. This happened one day in the middle of the afternoon – when I had already been there many days without food and water, and the sun was so strong that it made the matter of my thinking mind evaporate. With no thoughts available, I just watched the long ascension that the green spider made toward my chest. The closer she got to my chest, the stronger was my awareness that she knew exactly what she was doing and that I was about to receive a gift.

Once she stood still right in the center of my chest, I felt like I was falling into a deep well of light where I could hear her delicate, sharp voice speaking to me: "I am going to show you the power of your heart." Immediately after she spoke, I clearly saw myself standing on a field with a baseball bat in my hand, and the pitcher ready to throw the ball. "Does the bat go to the ball or does the ball go to the bat?" she asked me. "The ball goes to the bat," I answered without thinking. In my vision, I saw a big light in my chest where I could feel the weight of the little insect spirit that was helping me, and lines of light were traveling from my heart all the way through my arms into my hands and all the way through my legs into my feet. Then, without making any effort, completely relaxed and confident, I hit the ball. "When you have your heart awake, like now," the spider told me, "all that you want comes to you without you making too much effort. This is how we spiders hunt, never going after our prey; we just build a web and all that we need comes to us."

The implications of this teaching were very big for me. At that time in my life, I really needed to learn that too much effort was as bad as not making any effort. I needed to learn that it did not make me less of a man to develop the feminine magnetic wisdom, especially when I knew how much I could exhaust myself and others every time my electric masculine energy moved excessively and in a forceful way. It was about time for me to be able to trust in my heart's capacity to call and attract all that I needed and wanted without forcing myself or anyone else. As a man, I realized it was time for me to let go of the forceful, masculine way of getting what I needed – for me, for my family, or for the world around me. I became very interested in learning about the ways of the feminine nature. I wanted to stop my way of going to work like someone who is going to war, and for this to be my small contribution to the healing and change of the world where our children are growing up.

Men who have a strong masculine nature have a natural inclination toward certain attitudes – such as conquering, protecting, and fiercely fighting for something important to them. I don't mean to say that there is something inherently wrong with these masculine tendencies. If Nature put them in us, then they must be useful for something, and for sure in our communities sometimes they are. But they need to be in balance and not overused, or they end up crushing the soft movements of the feminine nature that permeate all the spheres of human life. I learned from my Lakota *Ate* (father) about how his ancestors took care of creating this balance. One day, he shared with me about what Lakota warriors did in the old days when coming back to their village after having been in battle. They had been brave and knew, when leaving home, that they may not come back alive. So when being gifted with the opportunity to return alive back to their people and their families, they had to take care of something really important: they had to leave the warrior outside the village. The way they took care of this, my father told me, was by having someone wipe off the warrior paint from their faces. In this ritual, the paint that marked their faces before going into battle was totally removed with prayers and songs. The man would then be freed from the warrior, and the warrior wouldn't bring his bravery, his trauma, or his fighting skills into the village.

At home, the women were in charge of the collective well-being of the community, making sure that everyone – from the children to the elders – is being cared for and nourished. Warriors turned into gentle men who respected and nourished the heart of the women.

What the spider taught me worked in that same way for the warrior in me: it wiped away a certain image I had of myself as a man and increased my respect for all that is feminine. Being immersed in sacred time when it happened, I not only had the chance to learn but also to change my perception – of myself in this case – which gave me the power to continue improving my behavior.

At least now I am more aware of what happens when the illness of spiritual forgetfulness invades a village: the clearest symptom is that the balance between masculine and feminine forces gets lost; men abuse women, women abuse men in their own fashion, and everyone forgets to take care of Mother Earth.

THE HEALING POWER OF VISION QUEST

When someone came to get me after many days alone on the hill, I cried because I didn't want to go. The best food and shelter I ever had were there in the wild, exactly where I was, with the sun, the moon, the winds, and the spiders.

Very difficult ceremonies – like fasting alone on a hill – provide us with the resources to remember the well-being of our people and the world in which we live. In these ceremonies, years of human routine are severely interrupted. Everything stops when we stop eating, talking to people, and sleeping under a roof for a few days. It is for sure a ceremony of life renewal, like most ceremonies we do. After having been on the hill crying for a vision, we have a real chance to start a fresh new life. This is how our Indigenous grandfathers and grandmothers taught us to create and change our reality: interrupting the course of our life and looking for a gift of Spirit in the form of a vision. The vision anchors our present reality in the possibilities that come from the future, freeing us from having to dwell in the past and be conditioned by its endless consequences.

The development of sacred talents like vision and spiritual wisdom is not just a personal journey; it is not just a matter of growing personal power or having personal spiritual satisfaction. It is surely not something to show off. As clearly seen among the humble people of the tribal worlds still alive today, the healthy relationships of the members of a community are preserved by the use of these sacred powers. When there is awareness, people do not step on each other's toes that much. A fluid and harmonious cooperation of everybody's talent is possible when living and working together, thanks to each one going through spiritual training.

When the bond of community members is mature enough, they develop sort of a collective mind. It happens that different members of the extended family start visiting the same dreams, or that their dreams and visions received in ceremonies match each other like pieces of a puzzle. We believe that our ancestors did not rely on just one exceptional visionary person to find a direction for their future and design their way of life. Even when such gifted individuals have existed, they relied mostly on the interconnectedness of everyone's minds and hearts. Little by little, the pieces of the puzzle come together, with even the children at times providing them, and the community grows strong and beautiful under a spiritual guidance collectively received.

Many years of work and sometimes more than one generation are necessary to arrive at this level of collective maturity. Before this, the gifted seers alone carry the weight of the responsibility for guiding the group. If they are men, outsiders may see the development of a patriarchal society; if they are women, it may be seen as a matriarchal society. This is truly missing the point. What people are really looking for is not as narrow as a choice between two options; people are really looking to be like Nature itself, where the masculine and the feminine and all that is born from their union have the same chance to give their singing voice to the jungle, where the union of all the voices in one big song is what we call "our life," "our village," "our world."

Many of us who do these ceremonies are seeing the same truth from different angles: to be a patriarchal or matriarchal society is not the main issue. What really matters is whether or not we are spiritually awake. When the little green spider woke me up, I realized that as a man I can learn to be guided by a feminine principle. And I suspect that it is the same for a woman; sometimes she can be guided by a masculine principle. These are sacred universal principles that guide all of us, and they belong to a place beyond the cultural norms and beliefs that differentiate men and women.

12

THE TEACHINGS
OF THE SNAKE

Aware that the time of the black jaguar has arrived
and that it is time for us to change in order to
continue living, I want to take the reflections in
these pages further, to the place where I find the
greatest difficulty and the greatest potential for us
human beings: the relationship between man and
woman.

Having full trust in the goodness of each other's
heart is the agreement that sustains human relationships. Most of us know what happens once this
agreement is broken and the relationship has to be
based on rules, politeness, or domination by the
strongest. Under these forms of behavior that create
a superficial appearance of wellness, the heart is
unhappy and feeling lonely. In my case, as in the case
of many others, this condition ended in divorce for
me and my wife, a truly painful experience.

Because of my own experience, I paid more attention to what was happening to people around me
regarding their love life and found out this problem

was truly epidemic. And beyond that, because of some understanding I had gathered in my work as a healer, I started seeing clearly how much the future of humanity depends on the healing of the separation between the genders.

This is not just a problem between one man and one woman – who could be our father and mother. Today, this is a social condition with its own role in history. The history of the constant breaking and repairing of the relationship between the genders goes hand in hand with the history of war. In times ruled by wars, the warriors – usually men – take over the control of their society to make sure they can enforce the strategies that will keep their people and their business safe. They become the power, and power can always be abused or misused when spiritual guidance and feminine wisdom are left out.

In times ruled by wars and with the help of intolerant religions, men were led to see women as a distraction, as the possible tempting snakes. And women were led to see themselves in the same way. The snake became a symbol of evil, and she was feared and killed wherever she was found. As a result, the space where men and women used to fill their hearts with sweetness and compassion was replaced by a sexuality contaminated by guilt and fear. Once the space where couples practiced the total opening of their hearts became obscure, the most accessible way of awakening compassion in daily life was debilitated.

For Indigenous people, snakes are sacred and this kind of thinking never existed before the arrival of the conquistadors. This may be why so many of our ancestors were called savages or devil worshipers. Our ancestors were just sexually healthy and innocent; and this was ruined when they were told that there was something wrong with having sexual organs and sexual appetite.

Our ancestors held sacred the moment of love. They knew that the deepest aspect of the partnership formed by men and women grows in the time of loving each other, the sacred time when the ego gets killed by love. They knew how much we all need this "medicine." When masculine and feminine energies fuse, refined vibrations are generated, and these have the power to elevate as light. When the opportunity for this profound connection of love is damaged, relationships are weakened. When the partnership between men and women becomes weak, then families suffer, communities break, and the entire nation becomes weak. Human strengths such as willpower, compassion, and the seeking of freedom are kept alive when people are inspired by love and there is blending of feminine and masculine qualities. Those who live deeply in love with the fullness of life are capable of fighting for what they care for with all that they have.

Seeing how the world is now and how much it has to change for us to be healthy again, many of us feel that it is very necessary to work on creating a new trust in the relationship between the genders. From this new trust, men and women will be fully open to love again and, starting from the place of their intimate love, will grow multiple forms of cooperation.

As of today, the deterioration of the relationship between men and women is still the source of much illness and destruction on Earth. Not knowing how to arrive at the longed-for experience of pure love and profound intimacy, frustration and deep resentment grow in the human soul. In too many cases, these emotions turn into aggressive behavior and severe illness of the mind and body.

Unless we heal this condition and allow the feminine principle to enter the hearts of both men and women, some men will continue wanting to live for fighting and conquering. There will be more wars. Economic, military, and religious warlords will continue running our society, and a false masculine force will continue being the image of power for most human beings.

MY ENCOUNTER WITH THE WISE SNAKE

The teaching that I received from the spider made me look at myself in a very deep way. In a world mostly run by forceful masculine minds, I started becoming fully aware of how the feminine nature was getting crushed. I became aware of my unconscious participation in the disrespect towards the feminine as my love for Her was growing more and more every day. Because of my work of healing and rituals, I had to be in ceremony very often, and that meant being with Her. She is the medicinal herbs;

she is the talking stone; she is the sweet smell of the healing smokes; she is the crying voice of the sick ones; she is the blue star that guides us and the fresh water that touches our mouth bringing back to us the memory of our health. Over and over again, I came back to a place where I recognized Her infinite beauty and went on my knees when seeing the power of Her unconditional love.

With the help of a few years of intense suffering and the guidance of some good friends and Elders, I was able to recognize that the same conditions that caused the divorce with the mother of my children created my separation from the feminine nature that I had come to love so much. I really wanted to remedy this, so I prayed for help.

The most amazing thing is that Spirit already knew what was going to happen to me before it happened, and the help started coming even shortly before the divorce. I was helped to start changing my perception of the relationship between men and women while doing a Vision Quest in the desert of New Mexico. The useful insights I received in that experience I now want to share with all those needing help as I did during those years.

I had been sitting under a tree for many days without food and water. Crying for a vision with a *Cannunpa* – sacred pipe – in my hands, very thirsty and tired, I was using the little energy I had left to fight with the flies that kept testing my attention and patience. Realizing how distracted I was, I straightened my back and prepared myself for finding my silence again. Soon it all got better. Even the flies stopped bothering me. It was then that I saw, at the top of a small, nearby tree, a large pink snake looking at me. We stared at each other's eyes for a while, which made me feel a deep desire to fall asleep. I made the effort not to do so, and then I felt more awake than ever. Thoughts from the snake's mind started appearing in my mind, along with some very clear images.

She started with a very strong statement: "In the beginning, all humans, boys and girls alike, are born as females." As I kept giving her my full attention, she put thoughts in my mind that explained how later girls naturally grow up to become women. This happens when they start being called by the female power of the moon to whom they are kin, and also by the queen of femininity, Mother Earth, whose magnetism absorbs their menstrual blood. Even when young girls may benefit from certain teachings and from going through a rite of passage, their most powerful initiation happens naturally as their bodies develop into womanhood. But for boys to become men, more awareness is needed; it is not enough to have their first wet dreams and realize that now they are capable of making babies. Boys need to consciously choose to become men and work on it.

We all begin our lives inside our mother's body; we all start our lives being part of her, being her, a feminine being. Real manhood, as I understood with the help of the snake, is only the result of work and learning; it cannot be taken for granted.

Awakening in my mind clear memories of my childhood, she helped me to see what happens when we are boys and teenagers. We keep watching the girls grow up, becoming women as the feminine beings that they are naturally. We watch how the mysterious power that started dwelling in their feminine bodies grows so clearly every day, while we, originally feminine but equipped with undeveloped masculine potential, constantly need to seek references from our father and other role models to help us grow to be men.

Boys need to be taught and initiated in order to become men. The snake helped me to see how most nations around the world are in a human crisis due to the lack of initiations and teachings for boys to become men. So strongly seeking examples of masculinity, boys are receiving false models, full of violence and arrogance, born from the media and the problems of the male adults. Clearly and without beating around the bush, the snake told me that not all those who have a penis are real men.

With the snake's help, it started to become clear to me that in a society with a lack of real models of masculinity, most boys grow up with insecurities. These insecurities often appear when in the presence of girls who are becoming strong in their feminine nature. If this condition continues at a more advanced age, a mysterious, strong, and attractive young woman could feel like a threat to a youngster who still has not found how to be a man. So, somehow, he wants to conquer her. He wants to prove that he is also strong, much stronger than her. From here, very often two forms of male conduct are born: the way of the abusive male and the way of the male who is a sucker.

The abusive males use their physical and mental strength to overpower women and put them under themselves. The suckers repeat with their girlfriends and wives the same patterns that they learned as babies to get their mothers' attention and milk. Both the abusive male and that one who depends on the comfort of "his mother's milk" are males who haven't become men yet, no matter how old they are. The abusive one is really afraid of his lack of personal power, so he needs to constantly put down the females to feel that he is the one who rules. Aggressive demonstrations of power and superiority are his well built defenses. And the man who still needs to suck energy from his mother is a manipulative man, a spoiled kind of man who feels entitled to be served and who gets mad when not given what he wants.

Many men who seem to be very powerful suffer from these weaknesses.

It is sad enough that women have to put up with these two different kinds of male behavior. But it is not only the women who have to endure this; it is also our Mother Earth. All the damage done to our Mother has been directed by men who suffer from one of the conditions just described or from a combination of both. These men first started suffering from some insecurity, as is normal for most boys, but they did not have the fortune of receiving the right teachings for becoming men. They became efficient at what they always do: dominating and exploiting the gifts of the feminine. We all can see this as we watch how the Earth's wild powers have been crushed or tamed, and how the Earth's juicy fruits are being sucked until the last drop by non-initiated men.

SHE SPEAKS ABOUT WOMEN

After seeing what the snake was showing me and feeling shocked by the truth in it, I started making my own conclusions about the condition of men – and also started to feel guilty about it. She read my mind and moved down the little tree towards me, stopping at a very short distance from my head.

By making this aggressive move, she stopped my thoughts; then she asked me to look at the condition in which many women are living. My mind became filled with battles scenes from the different European wars: millions of soldiers dying and millions of women becoming widows, having to raise their children alone under the most difficult conditions, feeling the need to develop some masculine strength to be able to survive. I was also shown scenes of women who decided to increase their power after getting tired of being with an abusive man. The power that they grew in order to defeat him was masculine. Then, I saw a clear image of a modern European type of woman, less feminine, more masculine. At this moment, the snake told me that the energy of women is so flexible and resourceful that if necessary they can grow a "man" within themselves. The lack of men or the lack of men who could be trusted forced a great number of women to do this. These women then passed on their new "strengths" to the girls of the generations that came after them.

Unfortunately, the "man" that a woman can grow within herself isn't a real man either.

FALSE MASCULINE, WEAK FEMININE

Thanks to the light that the sacred snake was shining on some blind spots of my mind, I had a very deep realization on that day of Vision Quest. I could see that both men and women have been promoting the development of a false masculine force, which is just the external manifestation of their image of power. Nowadays, everyone feels entitled to be powerful in the family and in the world, and the false masculine is ruling. I was able to understand that we are not really suffering from an excess of the authentic sacred masculine principle; we are suffering from an excess of a false masculine force.

Stopping the destruction of our world is what is at stake now. The destruction of the Earth is only possible when not enough men are man enough to stand up and do something to stop it. The world isn't really suffering from an excess of masculinity; there is just a serious lack of authentic masculinity. We are not in the condition we are in because our culture became patriarchal and the masculine dominated everyone. What happened is that the masculine force now dominating the world is heartless and abusive; it is war oriented, out of balance, and sick. This kind of dominant masculine force is a pale expression of the true potential that lives within the sacred masculine principle, which is honorable and beautiful.

If the actions of men were the true expression of the sacred masculine, it wouldn't be a problem to have them provide, as a humble service, the direction of our society. It isn't at all wrong to allow the masculine to govern, when men are not afraid of women and willing to co-govern with them. When afraid of women, the man who is not fully developed will either tend to be submissive to her or try to get her out of the way, missing the opportunity of the most valuable relationship of cooperation. Only when men defeat their own insecurities and become solid as a tree can they open their mind to the flow of a woman's feminine intelligence without feeling threatened by it.

Humanity is also in need of the return of the real feminine principle.

The healing of our world requires the talents of a type of feminine intelligence that was neglected when seeking power became so important. This type of intelligence – intuitive and wise – is rooted in the Earth, in the heart, in the way the waters move. The purpose of its existence is to take care of life by recognizing the most essential needs of living creatures. I have observed in my grandmothers and sisters how this recognition always happens in the present moment by using awareness that comes from feeling, without the need of linear thinking. This type of feminine intelligence is so fast, vast and round that rational explanations seem very slow and limited in contrast. We all need the service that this intelligence provides for us. It is sad to witness women choosing to develop the masculine intelligence, and allow their female powers to weaken. This is understandable, when the world, as it is today, rewards with success those who are intelligent in a more "masculine" way.

Feminine intelligence is more difficult to understand, at least for men, and especially in modern cultures that have distanced themselves from the primal feminine wisdom of the Earth. For Indigenous and ancient cultures of people who live very close to the Earth, it is the opposite: feminine intelligence, being closer to the mystery, is seen as being closer to the truth. The feminine principle has always been a source of fascination for tribal people who tirelessly explore it in their ceremonies and rituals. Mystery, as much as the intuitive feminine knowledge, is for Indigenous people a sacred source. Our rational knowledge does not seek to eliminate it.

GRANDMOTHER'S MEDICINE

From what I've learned in my travels deeply observing the ways of other cultures, I can say that, in most parts of the world, women used to be the heart of not only their own families but also of their entire communities. From their heart, the most grounded wisdom and intuitive intelligence were always offered for the benefit of the people. In some places, it is still like that; but the loss of the deepest feminine presence in the modern world runs at the same rate as the loss of trees in the forests. Nowadays, it is more difficult for many women to trust their intuition. To trust in the achievements offered by modern education is easier, which is reducing the presence of feminine intelligence in the world's communities.

Even in our Indigenous communities, we have fewer grandmothers like the ones of the old days who were so full of wisdom when giving orientation to the young ones. No matter how many braves and excellent men a community might have, they would never dispute the most elevated position and the most humble – the one of the grandmother. Wrinkled like a turtle, wise as the weaving of snakes, loving, sweet and funny, she is always the medicine that never fails: a source of balance for everyone.

Grandma's wisdom is not being heard as much as it used to be, so she is talking less. The loss is immense because grandmothers keep and pass on the memory of the ancestors.

Not listening to the wise grandmothers who are still with us is unfortunate enough; but, on top of that, little girls and young women in most parts of the world aren't trained anymore to become the wise grandmothers of the future. We are suffering a lack of the important help grandmothers can provide in a time of crisis like the one we are in today.

I am grateful to my grandma and to all those women who show the rest of us the greatest human power: the one that resides in the heart, and that they embody better than anyone else. The love of a woman can be so immense that I have no words to describe it. I am in awe when I see her take care of the ones she loves, nourishing them without conditions, doing things with such beauty, with such sweetness. Some of her mysteries are clear to me, others are deeply dark, and in both, I find all that is really enjoyable in life.

THE UNITY OF WOMEN AND MEN

As men who want to be real, we need to be trustworthy like the sun who never fails to appear in the morning. Then the women who are next to us may relax in their own waters and enjoy the complete flowering of their abundant feminine being. A man should learn from another man to be the Sun's child, to stay firm in the place from where he nourishes and nurtures the feminine, without allowing his own little needs and personal defenses to get in the way. The Sun, our cosmic teacher, never fails to appear in the morning. He is trusted and, because of this trust, life on Earth has balance. According to principles of physics, the Sun creates a curvature in space that allows the Earth to be in permanent motion, always remaining in orbit without becoming lost in the infinite universe. I believe women need us to be present, fully present, in a similar way.

The knowledge of the masculine rational mind is useful and necessary, but we don't need to be imposing what we think we know on everyone else. Rational knowledge is just the help we need to counter-balance the abundant, powerful, fluid, and unpredictable tides of the wild feminine nature. This unpredictably is beautiful; it is a manifestation of *Taku Wakan Skan Skan*, of "Something Sacred in Perpetual Motion" which sustains all life. But for most men, what is unpredictable can be difficult to handle. Therefore, when the world seems too big and out of control, rational knowledge serves us to make it look smaller, more ordered, and manageable. This is all good and useful; but, when afraid or arrogant, we overdo it. We know when we are overdoing it when we only listen to ourselves and to no one else.

Healthy masculine intelligence is a powerful balancing force in Nature; but its goal is not to annihilate the feminine or defeat the mystery. Nor do we want to get used to always reducing our world to something manageable, small, and mediocre. I believe this is why we always return to the ceremonial house, to the sacred fire, to sacred time, to the love of a woman, to the abyss of love, to the place where we release everything we know and jump, so that we never forget how immense our hearts and minds really are. We welcome the movements of Mystery, the magic times in which we flow without knowing but with trust. Feminine intelligence gives us intuition and feelings of certainty that sometimes are not easy to understand with our head, but which allow us to move with beauty, spontaneity, and lightness in the only moment that exists – the present moment.

Over the years, I have shared the teachings of the snake a few times with both individuals and groups. Most people seem to clearly understand the role of the female principle incarnated in the beautiful hearts of women; but people ask over and over again what is the role of men, incapable of seeing what a healthy man really looks like, as if this has become the most obscure reality in the human mind.

I say this is work in progress. It is going to take us some time to return to our true sacred masculine qualities; but there is something we need to do as soon as possible. The snake gave me the clue to understand this. Remember how the snake showed me images of millions of men dying or becoming incapacitated in endless wars? Remember how she made me notice what happens to the women at home who never saw their husbands return alive or who saw them return without their full physical or mental integrity? I take this as the clue she gave me to guide me on my way back to myself. We men need to complete our return to our women, become a gift for them, real men. We need to come back home from battle, and like the warriors of the past, wipe the war paint off our faces before we enter their sacred space.

13

GOOD THOUGHTS ARE BORN IN THE HEART

Someone who instructed me and played a very important role in my life as a teacher, spiritual guide and mother was Mrs. Adela. I met her in the place where she worked everyday as a healer, seeing people who mostly needed help with very severe illnesses. Surprisingly, her workplace was an office inside a car repair garage in the most polluted and noisy avenue in downtown Lima. In that first meeting we had, it never crossed my mind that this mechanic's garage – full of engines, smoke, and noise – could become the temple where I would be given the opportunity to learn, grow, feel true spiritual peace, discover myself, and endure the most merciless attacks on my very stubborn ego.

From the first day, Mrs. Adela and I experienced a deep recognition of each other's spirit. Being a very experienced *seer*, she must have seen much more than I could. Since our first conversation, she knew why I was there and what potential there was for my future; but she didn't say that much or try to convince me of anything. She just opened the door for me, and only if I was aware of what was being offered would I cross it, using my own will. A few months later I became her apprentice, and a couple of years later I became her co-worker, sharing the big load of humble people in need of unconditional help that came to see her.

I remember the first time when I laid my hands on the body of a sick person. It happened during one of the Thursday evening sessions when about a hundred people gathered at her office. In the span of a few hours, surrounded by Mrs. Adela and her helpers, the participants came one at a time to lay down in the center of the room to receive spiritual healing. There was always singing, and there were powerful sacred spirits in the room. Among the people, there were many who had cancer or other fatal diseases, so the atmosphere felt strong and delicate at the same time. I was just there watching how tirelessly this woman took care of the sick ones and treated each one like a son or a daughter, no matter how old they were. She was sharp in her spiritual senses, always knowing how to handle every situation. I was there sitting among the people, not because I was sick, but because I liked the feeling of the sacred energy that vibrated so strongly in that room. Suddenly, Mrs. Adela, who seemed to be dealing with a difficult case, asked me to come and help. Taken by surprise, I just stood up and looked at her with the expression of someone who doesn't have a clue what to do. She looked at me without saying a word, and I understood what she meant:

"Just do it." At the end of the meeting, she smiled at me and said I had touched the person's body in the right place and in the right way. I had no idea what she meant, but was happy to hear it.

It must have been beginner's luck – or that I was taken by such surprise that my ego did not have time to figure out how to interfere with what my spirit knew. But the next few meetings when I helped with the healing, I did not feel as good as the first time. Nervous and tense, I had doubts about my capacity to really offer something to the people there who believed so much in us. So one night, I decided to be honest and spoke to Mrs. Adela about my feelings, and she told me not to worry. "Just do it from your heart," she said. Nothing else. Not too long after, I had the honor of meeting one of the Elders, one of Mrs. Adela's teachers, and I asked him the same question hoping to get a more elaborate answer. He knew what Mrs. Adela had told me and said it again, just adding a couple more words: "If you do it from your heart, you will never make a mistake."

Mrs. Adela and her teachers, who then became my guides, had a deep knowledge about the art of healing, including various healing techniques and the use of medicinal plants. But they did not start by teaching me that. The most important part of the art of healing is where you put your mind and your heart when you are at service. This is an inner movement, invisible to the outside world, that one can only do alone. Therefore, they started teaching me by leaving me alone with my questions, forcing me to act on the spot without thinking and with total precision whenever my help was needed, very often in life or death cases.

When I needed to know something, Mrs. Adela always gave me the same answer: "Know it in your heart." Very quickly, I learned that she also meant that once I had felt and known something in my heart, I had to act immediately and without a doubt. "To doubt is a sin," she said to me so often, as if she was joking; but she was serious. Another day, when she saw I was having a very hard time trying to relax and trust in the spiritual source from which I was being guided, she told me: "The Elders say that doubt is the only sin that exists." It was all clear now: what they were telling me is that our own spirit always knows what to do, out of wisdom and natural compassion. What we need to learn is to observe ourselves with pure honesty, so we do not allow any other part of our humanness to take over and interfere. I accepted this task. I observed myself with honesty and moved to the right place within myself when it was time to serve others. This became my practice and discipline.

I accepted being put in a situation where I had no choice but to trust my heart and my spirit and to learn to stop putting so much trust in my head's intelligence, which I realized was a tool in the hands of my ego. So many times, my ego tried to win at least one battle to prove it was right about something; but I was always disarmed and defeated by Mrs. Adela's common sense, which always had the power to touch the deepest truth with the utmost simplicity. I observed that this wisdom she had was somehow rooted in her love and care for the people and the sacred spirits who guided us just as much as my intelligence was rooted in my ego. The freedom of her heart and mind which made it so easy for her to fluidly resolve the most complicated issues inspired me; I wanted to be able to be that free, fluid and simple myself. For the next ten years, I didn't leave her side.

Later, at the end of my twenties, I met the men who guided me and authorized me to work with traditional Indigenous ceremonies, and they acted in exactly the same way as Mrs. Adela did. Guardians of the traditions they were passing on to me, the Elders and older brothers never tried to be intermediaries between me and the truth. They always encouraged me to discover the truth on my own, with my own heart. Loyal to the way that is traditional for Indigenous people, those who instructed me didn't try to educate me; they left me alone on a hill, they gave me medicine, they played tricks on my ego, and mostly, they touched my little heart with their big hearts.

When I was ready to learn something, they put me in situations where they knew I would learn by myself. More than being an authority superior to my own will, they made everything possible to assist me in my awakening. Even at the risk that my will would never emerge, they never interfered with the destiny that I was forging for myself. This is the level of respect that the guides and Elders of the old days had, and I was fortunate to find those still like them.

A HEARTLESS PATH

Nowadays, I see millions of people around the world allowing others to govern their thoughts. So many people are used to empowering intermediaries that give them a filtered truth, instead of using their own vision and feeling. When there is a need to know the truth, education and information, born from external sources, play a much stronger role than vision and feeling born from within.

Most modern forms of education and information nourish the head's intelligence – and in a masculine way only. The heart is not touched. As a result, for a long time it has been acceptable for most of humanity to have the head lead the way, governing the heart. This is the same as allowing a soldier to command a general or a computer to command the one who is using it.

There is so much access to information. It must be confusing to have so much information available. As a result, it is easy to lose connection to the simple truth. There is so much high-speed technology, so many scientific discoveries, and yet the highly educated modern man has as his most powerful achievement putting the entire planet at risk of extinction. Considering that this is the planet that our children will inherit, this "high intelligence" looks more like total foolishness to me. Something is clearly missing in the minds of people of the modern society.

Our Elders say that good thoughts begin in the heart. Nowadays, we see too much knowledge without wisdom, too much intelligence without heart.

In the world ruled by the conquerors with their great enterprises, there is no place for listening to the commands of the heart or to follow the mysterious motion of the feminine principle. Everything has to be controlled, quantified and calculated from the head so that results are achieved and there are no undesirable surprises. Feminine intelligence has become less important and the voice of the feminine is not being heard.

I am grateful for the many years I spent alongside Mrs. Adela, who guided me on my spiritual path. Being close to her gave me a chance to learn to appreciate feminine intelligence and to recognize that walking the way of the heart was my true choice.

Now that we live in an unpredictable time that is going to be full of surprises, the old masculine and controlling ways of thinking are going to prove to be too slow. Catching the wave of change requires the awakening of a much more open mind: the mind that dwells in the heart. How can we do this? Where is the greatest opportunity for the development of a flexible mind full of the capacities that feminine intelligence offers?

THE MIND OF THE SPIRIT

The masculine mind moves like electricity, looking for connections, looking for an outlet; it moves forward. The feminine mind moves like a magnet, circulating around its own center; like a spider with her web, it waits for what is needed and feels the gift when it arrives.

The human mind, living under the pressures of the human condition, is always busy, electric, seeking solutions. But this is not the only mind we have. We also have the mind of our spirit, which is more of a feminine nature, a spiritual magnet attracting help from the source, from the Mind of the Universe.

The sages of the ancient times discovered that in order to have wisdom, balance and will and to become a true complete human being, it is necessary to activate both minds: the human mind and the mind of the spirit. In the moment of receiving *understanding*, the mind of the spirit commands the human mind.

What my Elders taught me, and what I have confirmed with my own experience so many times, is that the connection with the mind of our spirit – the wise mind – happens through the heart, not through the head. Then, after the heart has received *pure understanding* from the mind of our spirit, it can pass the feeling to the human mind, whose job is to translate it into clear thoughts.

The connection between the heart and the mind of the spirit is nourished in the *dreamtime*, when we pray in ceremony, when we sing and dance sacred movements, when we experience meditation and true silence.

Nowadays, most people are taught in school to use only their head and their human mind; the mind of their spirit is dormant or has very little activity. I believe this is one of the causes for the lack of wisdom that allows the current state of humanity to continue its course, with suffering and hunger continuously growing without impediment.

When solutions for our problems become really urgent, we access the forces of Creation with the mind of our spirit. Creation always comes to the human world from the spirit world. Call it a dream, a vision, an inspiration, a miracle, or high intelligence, creative capacities are always the gift of the light.

Our spiritual mind needs to be active and our heart open to receive the sacred energy of the gift of creation. The sacred power of creation lives in seeds of light that we store in our heart. *Munay*, the will of the heart where these gifts of the light dwell, can grow and become very powerful.

Connecting our human mind with the mind of our spirit is about becoming available to the natural wisdom of the Universe. Truth, sacred creative power and divine intervention are always present around us, everywhere, so abundantly that they are truly limitless. The foolishness of humans today is to not make ourselves available to receive it, always running away from it, getting occupied with excessive planning, excessive thinking, and excessive effort. Too much effort is as bad as no effort; it creates the conditions for lack of silence and lack of time for what is really important. Most modern humans, including beautiful people with the best intentions, are trying to resolve everything without taking the time to really listen, without being available to respond to a call from Spirit at any moment. Those who make themselves available receive instructions and guidance directly from the source.

THE WAY OF THE HEART

There is a kind of profound understanding that makes it possible to feel the truth about things and beings. This understanding happens in the heart first, and then it moves up to the head. It is the big heart that produces sweet and nourishing fruits, while a big head demands and consumes all the energy of the moment as it strives to find perfection.

Among our Indigenous Elders, there are still those who practice a science that is rooted in the heart. Having their being anchored in their heart, they can travel very far on the paths of the Mystery and then come back with a gift. They travel throughout the universe until they find a good medicine or a good vision for the future. Their source is the vast mind of Spirit, not the limited human mind.

For those who want to practice it, there is still another method for getting knowledge, different than the method of the head, another science which is very ancient.

The sacred ceremonies that open our heart and help us find vision are part of the scientific method of ancestral tribal nations. Most of the medicinal plants used today for curing severe illnesses were discovered through this method. The plant told someone who had the gift of vision what she could heal. And then, the plant was not only used but respected and given offerings of gratitude. In the Indigenous scientific method, knowledge is always accompanied by wisdom, and the head is always accompanied by the heart.

Wisdom comes from Spirit; it is the knowledge given directly by Spirit, as simple and certain as the word of an Elder. Human knowledge alone, without having wisdom by its side, is always inconclusive; a step beyond it there is always the unknown, which makes doubts always present.

The scientific method of modern men is only in search of knowledge and founded in doubt. It is because of doubt that modern science can continue making steps into the unknown. The Indigenous scientific method, on the other hand, is founded in certainty as it comes from a state of pure consciousness more than from a series of thoughts.

States of doubt create a lack of confidence and a sense of separation. Certainty is a magnet; it is a state of pure confidence that creates unity. Doubt weakens us and serves us as an excuse to be lazy, slow, indecisive, and to justify mistakes. Certainty makes us stronger; it inspires us to take action and to be immediately responsible for the consequences.

Those who work with the method of doubt are like someone who shoots many arrows to see which one will hit the target. Those who work with the method of certainty of the heart have the discipline of someone who has only one arrow and only one moment between life and death. This is the moment of sacred power, the moment when the door is open and the choice has been made, the sacred time when all is possible. This mysterious time is the one used by Indigenous people to do "scientific research."

Doubt is the way of the head. Certainty is the way of the heart.

Thinking too much is a vice that is hard to release. This vice is rooted in the satisfaction that the ego feels from recognizing itself as being smart. To doubt is another vice rooted in our emotional center which gets satisfied by its own torments. A tormented emotional center acts like an addict; it is not interested in being healed or in being replaced by the peace that lives in the silence of Spirit.

Those who love deeply and want to take care of what they love decide to be disciplined. I learned from my Elders that repetition of a routine is not discipline. Real discipline is the practice of constantly paying attention in the present moment. One who is disciplined seeks, like a skilled hunter, to capture the moment of certainty. His or her life becomes a series of consequences generated from acts of power born in moments of certainty. Thanks to this kind of discipline, a huge amount of energy is accumulated in the center of one's will. This stored energy gives us the chance of becoming solid people with great *Munay*, great compassion and willpower centered in the heart.

Our heart is connected to the heart of Mother Earth, and Her heart is connected to the heart of the Universe. In the Universe, everything is connected, and all the hearts are bound by threads of light. From each heart pour rivers of blood that are life itself. Humans, animals, and trees have the same colored blood. Red is the color of the energy of the place where the Universe is constantly being born. Those who recognize themselves as part of the universal web can feel in their heart what is good for the continuity of life and what is harmful to the balance of all. In the end, everyone knows the truth. Memory lives within the spirit that flows in our blood. The access to this memory and the experience that we have when the state of amnesia is over is what Indigenous people call vision.

14

THE TEACHING OF THE BEAR

Near Telluride, a town in the mountains of Colorado, I was told that there lives a white man who goes out to hunt a bear every year. I have great admiration for the courage of this man who dares to approach the bear with just a bow and arrow. A rifle would give him a great advantage over the bear, but still he chooses a bow and arrow, which gives him and the bear equal power to take down the other. For two years in a row this hunter came home with a bear killed by his arrow; but things changed the third year. A very particular bear approached the man seemingly putting himself in reach of his arrow; then, at the crucial moment, the bear skillfully moved making the hunter miss his shot.

The bear continued playing with him for a few days, until the hunter returned home frustrated and without his trophy. A year after he went back to look for the same bear. When he arrived to the area where he knew he could find him, the bear was waiting for him. Like the year before, the bear would always make the man miss his shot. Then, suddenly, the bear stood still in a position where it would be impossible for the man to miss his shot. The hunter pointed his arrow at him and when ready to release the mortal shot, he had a powerful realization: killing the bear would end their relationship. He became aware of how much he had enjoyed this interaction with the bear, so he put down his bow and arrow.

The people who know this man told me that now every summer he goes back to the same place looking for the same bear – not to kill him, just to stalk him and enjoy this powerful relationship. The bear, great doctor and master of the mountains, showed him a different way of doing things, and the man, who had his heart awakened, was able to recognize the opportunity.

People of Indigenous cultures have among their Elders those who act like the bear of Telluride. By example, the Elders teach that to own what we want or love is not most important: most important is cultivating good relationships.

In a world ruled by competition, men and women like to win and collect trophies. To own what one wants is considered a success, and those who prove that they can succeed feel powerful and safe.

Tribal people weren't interested that much in owning or possessing anything or anyone, regardless of its usefulness. They understood that when possessing something or someone we end up consuming it to the last drop, sucking all its mystery and beauty; and then, when nothing is left, we need to go and conquer something or someone else. This is seen as rude behavior, poor and inelegant, a way of over-consuming what life offers to us, a way of mistreating what we find in our path.

We don't want to exterminate all that we find that we like, nor all that we find that we don't like. We want to live nourishing lives, keeping relationships that are always fresh, not allowing them to become moth-eaten in the drawer of our personal possessions. Not being able to keep alive what one already possesses, there is always a craving to have more, and the same story happens again and again.

WHERE ARE YOU?

Something about Indigenous mentality that makes me enjoy it without limit is its strong connection to the feminine principle. A beautiful example is how Runasimi (Quechua) speakers say "thank you." Actually there isn't a word that can literally be translated as "thank you," but there is an expression that conveys the feeling of gratitude in a very poetic way. In the area of Cusco where I have relatives and friends, what we say to express gratitude is "*Urpiyay Sonkoyay*," which means "my little heart a little dove." Men and women alike use this expression, which emphasizes the need to let the other know how our heart is vibrating, instead of the need to be polite and formally say thank you. The feminine nature is interested in, more than anything else, the truth and depth of the feelings that nourish relationships.

When nourishing relationships is the priority, people develop a mentality in which more important than asking "what is this?" is asking "where are you?" From a feminine perspective, connecting and cultivating relationships is much more important than possessing knowledge.

The modern culture transmitted by the educational system is one that deals with the unknown by defining it and converting it into something known. The question that always comes first when facing the unknown is "what is this?" Someone who is walking in the forest finds a strange insect and immediately asks "what is this?" After answering this question and making a definition of it, he feels satisfied. But having defined the insect does not really mean knowing the insect. The only way to really know something is having an intimate relationship with it.

Someone trying to investigate something as deep as the nature of the Bear Spirit starts asking, "What is a bear?" One researcher after another would define the bear according to their most recent discoveries. Others hear this definition and, if it is rationally acceptable, may assume to have understood and now possess the knowledge of what a bear is. However, their knowledge wouldn't be as deep as it is for someone who has actually been with a bear and has a close relationship with him. Therefore, more important than asking *what* the bear is, is asking *where* the bear is, seeking for experiences where its deepest nature can be seen in sacred motion. To make a definition of him stops his motion, and this is the same as killing him.

It is more important in the Indigenous mentality to know *where it is* than to know *what it is*. To ask *what it is* leads to the illusion of taking possession of something unknown and making it known, like a hunter taking his prey. To ask *where it is* makes you look for an encounter with it; it leads you to establish a relationship to the unknown being, object, or experience without possessing it.

Knowledge is very useful; but to preserve the healthy continuity of life, good relationships are more important than knowledge, and in the end, respectful and intimate relationships sustained through time naturally produce the most profound knowledge.

Scientific knowledge is, in many cases, some sort of mental ownership of things.

We can find many cases in which scientific knowledge becomes a good partner of commercial enterprises in which profit and success are the ultimate goal. In both science and business – and sometimes in love relationships too – the methodology is the same: first something is discovered, then it is studied, then it is owned, and then it is exploited to the maximum.

In Indigenous cultures, the scientific observer is not distant from what he observes but rather "dances" with it. In order to "study" the Earth, for example, the question is "where are you, Mother?" To know *where* Mother Earth is we need to make a deep connection with Her and feel where we are in relation to Her. We become aware, as we "dance" with Her body and spirit, of the effect that Her movements have on the state of our being – and ours on Hers.

Let's say I propose to someone that we strengthen our connection to eagles. What we do is go and look for an eagle, so we can talk to her directly. The first question is: "Where is the eagle?" This question, when made precisely and with a prayer, is an invocation that opens a door and allows us to enter into a higher state of consciousness. The experience of meeting the Eagle Spirit in the place where she dwells cannot be replaced by a definition of what she is. To define her could actually interfere with the potential of the relationship. When we believe that we already know something, we stop listening and the relationship stops growing.

The Indigenous scientists don't talk about what they are studying – as modern scientists would do – but rather talk *with* that which they are studying, and this is how they learn. While modern science is making a huge and valid effort to investigate and figure out the way the universal powers function, Indigenous people from all over the world have been having a relationship with them, dancing with them since remote times.

WHERE IS THE ONE YOU LOVE?

It is the same in love. It is more important for a couple to have real encounters than to keep trying to figure out who the other one is. For a profound encounter to occur, it is necessary to feel, even in the most subtle ways, *where* the other one is as well as *where* one is in relation to the other.

This feeling can only happen in the moment, given that we are energy in motion and our "locations" are changing all the time. Staying aware and available to flow with the movements created by constant changes, we keep dancing with the other. Awareness is, in this sense, the glue that sustains the state of togetherness. As long as the connection between two beings keeps being strengthened by their pure awareness of each other's presence, their dance flows beautifully; their union can always remain strong.

Those afraid of what is unknown about their partner seek tranquility by trying to understand the other and to be understood by the other. In doing this, they usually get stuck and cannot "dance" together anymore. This habit is the result of how modern intellectualism educates the mind, promoting the development of knowledge and the gathering of information as tools of power and control. These tools are mostly needed because of fear.

It is more important to have a real encounter in the moment than to spend days and days trying to understand the other or to be understood by the other. To deeply understand another takes a long time and cannot happen before taking a ride in a river of experiences. Meanwhile, it is healthy to allow ourselves to dance in the mystery, always sustaining the simple question: "Where are you?" and "Where am I in relation to you?" An answer to this question will not necessarily help to understand the other; it will help to really be present with the other, to be so close that the other can be seen.

One of the big traps that we can fall into is having the illusion of possessing the other – once we have put the other one in a box. When we possess something or someone, we kill its mystery. We stop asking "where are you?" assuming that the other one is always "with me" which also translates as "it is mine." This is pure laziness. When possessing things or people we take away their capacity to be in sacred motion and, as a result, we weaken the power of our own motion. In time, this not only makes us lazy, it also makes life boring.

In order to have a good relationship, it is better to let go of the other and to be open to meet again and again. We know from experience that a good relationship needs freedom, open doors, and equal power between the two parts. To respect each other's freedom is a strong way of becoming united; in this unity, there is the greatest opportunity for truly getting to know the other. On the other hand, to believe that someone belongs to you creates separation. When the separation occurs, many people experience that they perceive the other as a stranger, someone different than the one they thought they knew – which was actually the one they had made up in their mind. Like most people, I have gone through this and know well how it feels.

We should never stop walking like the "hunters" who constantly exercise their capacity to meet the spirit of what they want and what they love. Like the bear of Telluride, the secrets of life are playful and evasive, and thanks to this, our senses are kept sharp and our spirit awake. Would it be better to change the ways of Nature and have everything under our control?

A fascinating life is that of the hunters of moments. Those who live hunting moments cannot waste time wondering what it is they have beside or in front of them. Their courage allows them to first develop the relationship, leaving the understanding for later. They have to let go of the habit of having to understand and define everything in order to feel ready to make connections, to establish relationships. The hunters of moments need to be fluid and alert and do not want to lose their freedom by becoming slaves of their material or intellectual possessions. When becoming interested in something or someone, what they immediately do is become open to establishing a relationship. If there is time and opportunity to continue discovering the other, they also remain open to being discovered. They are always asking "where are you?" and honoring the fact that everything is in sacred perpetual motion. In the mentality of Indigenous people, this applies to scientific studies, love relationships, hunting, gathering, to the relationship with the Mystery and with all that interests us.

It is important to keep a good relationship with the powers and treasures of Nature. This is more important than materially or conceptually owning them. To respect the lives of others is a refined way of life; always seeking to meet their essence and to admire their beauty and power, especially when they are sources of nourishment for us. We encounter the powerful spirit of our food when it is a seed, when it is growing under the sun and the rain, when we harvest it, and even when we feel its flavor in our mouth. We keep seeking the encounter in ceremonies of celebration and gratitude with that which is part of us: potatoes, corn, buffalo, delicious fruits, bitter medicines, and fresh waters. And then we have another encounter with the energy of these earthly powers when we go back to work and feel the health and strength that they gave us. Full of this energy, now it is our turn to nourish them and help them grow again. In this way, the circle of life remains strong. We are them, and they are us. In our encounter with them, we find ourselves. Within ourselves, we find them continuing their life. There is one single universal power permanently flowing from one body to another. Where is it?

15

THE SENSE OF THE COMMON GOOD

In a place called El Mallin in Patagonia, Argentina, I had a beautiful experience where I clearly saw the power of humans cooperating with each other. A group of people had requested that we do an *Inipi* or sweatlodge ceremony, and for this, we needed to build a structure. This structure is a little, round, enclosed lodge made from tree branches; inside, around 20 people can sit together, singing sacred songs and praying in the intense steam generated by water poured over heated lava rocks placed in the center. The problem was that we only had an afternoon to do this work, and we had originally planned to use this time to do some other spiritual practices for developing our awareness. The solution to this dilemma suddenly became clear to me. I proposed to the group that the time of building the sweatlodge also be the time for doing our awareness work. I suggested that all of us, around 20 people along with some of their children, go to a beautiful place near the river and build the lodge together and without talking.

They had never built a sweatlodge before, and some were wondering how the instructions would be given, how we would make decisions and, in general, how we would organize ourselves without talking. In response, I told them that this was the challenge; we would have to pay attention as never before and flow together like in a dance, seeing the lodge form itself while we cooperated with each other. I also encouraged them to always do what they felt needed to be done, without asking and without doubt, and to never think that someone else would do it. Lastly, I recommended that anyone who saw someone in need of help just go and help immediately.

What for me started as an experiment to observe the true capacities of human beings, ended up being one of the most joyful experiences I have ever had. After two or three hours of working together in total silence, the sweatlodge was finished, perfectly built and ready for ceremony. What a beautiful ceremony that was! The energy we had left in the lodge as we worked in harmony was still vibrating and nourishing us while we were praying. It was a life-changing experience for us all to discover our human capacity to cooperate in such a powerful way. In this case, just by agreeing not to talk, the usual interferences were eliminated, and our true nature showed up. We not only accomplished our task, but every single person was feeling open and content.

In tribal and communitarian mentality, there is a "sixth sense" which eliminates the need for an excessive authority: the sense of the common good. When giving direction becomes extremely necessary in a community, leaders can be firm and strong; the rest of the time, they use their talents to activate among the people a sense of the common good. Different from the cultural mentality of "following the leader," the sense of the common good makes every member of a community responsible for the well-being and health of everyone.

The sense of the common good is simply the real "common sense." It awakes every time an individual has a conflict between what he "likes" or "wants," and what is good for the well-being of the members of his family or his extended family, his community. Sometimes one seems to sacrifice a personal desire for the well-being of everybody else; but this is not really a sacrifice because the well-being of everybody is one's own.

Happiness is not personal. We are really happy when we are open and happy with others and with everything. A sense of oneness with others is developed through this mentality, as if the community is one big person of which we are all a part.

It is a great relief to put the personal ego to rest and to feel like we have a heart much bigger than our own: the collective heart. Contrary to what the personal ego fears, giving ourselves to the well-being of a circle of life does not take away our freedom. What freedom can be more real than being able to love without fear? Only strong individuals have the necessary will to love like this, living in solidarity with others. Communities where strong relationships of solidarity are developed cannot be composed of followers or individuals who are weak in their personal will; only people with a strong core can live in this way.

THE CONSENSUS OF A HUMAN COMMUNITY

There is a powerful place where the choice between the path of cooperation and that of competition has to be made: the place of decision making.

In societies where decisions are made by consensus, issues are discussed until everybody agrees on what direction to take. While the voting system promotes separating in bands and aggressive competition for the majority of votes, the way of consensus requires a conscious effort to unite the minds and hearts of the people. In this way, issues are discussed until everyone agrees on the right decision. When a community engages in the discussion of a possible decision, it becomes pregnant and circular – and when it gives birth, the right decision shows its face. The feminine principle is energy in motion that circulates through the people and ends up provoking a natural outcome, one that is healthy and serves the common good.

Those who have the right to participate in decision making by consensus, far from being passive and opinionated spectators of their social reality, are mature individuals who make themselves actively responsible for the condition of their world.

Sometimes, a little bit of conflict before reaching consensus is healthy. A healthy conflict can be like an intense fire that allows its light to illuminate what was in the dark so it can be seen by all. This serves the common good, because there are occasions when the truth only appears after a conflict. As long as the truth is spoken and there are no ego competitions, conflict does not have to end up in verbal or physical violence.

Contrary to the common good is trying to win a conflict for a personal victory – a victory that will only serve our ego. One stops being medicine for the others when trying to become the main light in the center of the circle. Born from conflict or from prayer, the light always comes from the sacred fire of Spirit, and the rest of us sit around it. Wise leaders do not put themselves in the center and take the place of the sacred fire; instead, they can humbly see and express what the fire is saying.

Developing the sense of the common good is extremely useful and necessary in this time of renewal when difficulty and uncertainty about the future threaten to cloud our minds. Many questions can be quickly answered when using this sense. Fear will always lead us to isolate ourselves and stay defensive and confused. The sense of the common good leads us to work with others, staying open to discover the solutions that we can all find together. It is good to practice having little councils with those closest to us, making decisions by consensus. Hopefully, we will all engage in the larger council of the human race at this crucial time, and looking for the well-being of all, participate in making decisions that support change. Instead of watching the news every night to be told what is going on, we can all make the news together – really good news.

A HUMBLE WAY OF BEING

In Indigenous communities, councils are made up of mature men and women along with wise Elders. To complete a good circle, some "invisible people" are heard as well. On very important occasions, before or after the councils of the humans, very sacred ceremonies are made to pray, ask for help, and consult the sacred spiritual powers.

The sacred powers of Earth and Sky as well as of the ancestors are part of the Indigenous community. As members of our community and part of our life, they are also heard and included as part of the council. Decisions made by consensus also include the voice of the sacred powers. This is why our ceremonies are so important. In them, we activate our vision and our consciousness to feel the presence of the sacred powers and listen to how they respond to the call of our drums, our rattles, and our songs. We don't live alone in this world. We live with many sacred forms of life, and we owe respect to all of them: animals, trees, mountains, and the celestial powers that look down from above to the Earth. In this sense, it is normal to include them in decisions which affect their lives as much as ours. Their spirits show up to take care of us because they recognize that we are part of the same universal web, that there is a strong interdependence between all of us, and – to put it simply – because they feel for us.

Good relationships among ourselves, with all creatures and with the sacred powers is the foundation of a good way of life. From good relationships, endless and rich possibilities are born. A healthy relationship with the feminine nature, with our mother Pachamama, creates conditions for the endless birthing of abundant sources of good food and water for our people. The expression of our true gratitude and respect for Pachamama comes always before eating our food. We do not put ourselves above the spirit of the Earth or act as if we own Her, because relationships of superiority or inferiority are normally not healthy. It is important for us to always remember that the unity of the circle of life – and not humans – is the greatest power on Earth. We want to respect the natural order and intelligence that moves in the circle preserving the health and balance of all life, including our own. Within this order, each species plays a role that is important for the well-being of everyone else. Every form of life in the wilderness naturally practices the sense of the common good.

Given that life moves in a circle, the natural way energy is meant to circulate is a clue to the health of all. For thousands of years, we have been using our sacred instruments and our songs to nourish the sacred motion of life. The energy we move is offered to all beings and, after circulating, returns to us to bless and nourish us.

The role we humans play in the circle is the one of caretaker, like a gardener. There are many forms of life in the garden, and we have the capacity to take care of their health. We use our creative talent to produce beautiful and nourishing vibrations. We use that within ourselves which is luminous like the Sun to configure our world in ways that are delightful for the spirits watching us. But the gardener is not superior to the plants, animals, and waters he takes care of on this Earth. For without water and plants, there would be no gardener.

It is true that we have great talents that other species do not have. But the purpose of our talents is not that the other forms of life serve us. On the contrary, the inherent purpose of our talents is to serve others.

We have put much attention into observing and getting to know the powers and talents of other forms of life: plants, stones, animals, waters, fires, winds and mountains, as well as the Sun, the Moon and the stars. We recognize that all of them have capacities that we do not have and that, when we really pay attention, they become our teachers and our medicines.

This mentality of not feeling superior over other forms of life creates a natural humility among Indigenous people. Humility is considered a very refined way of being. Lack of humility, arrogance, or personal greatness are seen as very rude behavior in the houses of the Indigenous people. There is no merit in being humble either. Those who are humble are simply aware of the truth and are naturally serving the common good. They inherently know how to distinguish what is truly great and what is not. Greatness is always associated with the sacred. Because of their awareness of where the real power truly is, they do not dare to put themselves in the center of the world.

We call the unity of the great circle of life *Pachamama* in Runasimi and *Wakan Tanka* in Lakota. In the old days in Europe, it was called the Dragon – a great being made from the unity of many animals, like the snake, the eagle, the lion. This Dragon reminds me of the Sphinx of the Egyptians. In Egypt, Napoleon shot a cannon ball at the nose of the Sphinx as if wanting to stop her from breathing. In Europe, in earlier times, a knight named George was made a saint for killing the Dragon. For Indigenous people, these are very difficult things to understand. We see the death of the Dragon as a deep wound in our Mother's heart and as the end of the magic power that makes life beautiful. When the Dragon was killed, the powerful unity of the spirits of Nature as one large body was broken. The spirit of Nature was weakened, and a few humans could then rule above all beings. Since then, we are seeing a massive exploitation of the fruits of Mother Earth – with no other party having the power to oppose and stop it.

Did Napoleon grow up having a place within a circle? I wonder why Napoleon was the way he was, why he wanted to conquer the world. I wonder how he was treated by his father and his mother. Why did he need to become so important? It is really amazing what he did to prove that he was the strongest. So many men like him have put themselves in the center, in the place of power for a while. Losing their sense of the common good, they become so destructive for the world and for humankind. I am of the impression that these men, even if they like women, do not really love the feminine. Or perhaps they never had real contact with the feminine so they couldn't even see or recognize the power and beauty of its presence. Perhaps they never received what they needed from the feminine and became angry. I do not really know if they were aware of what they were destroying; but surely if they were, they must have felt the need to get the wild feminine power out of their way to become rulers of the world. The feminine, Pachamama, the Dragon, the Sphinx and women, can also get angry and destructive sometimes to shake us a bit, to wake us up. This feminine anger, when not born from pride or fear, is just a surprising manifestation of a very pure love. It is like the sacred black jaguar who serves as a fierce protector of the common good.

16

THE OTHER HALF
OF THE HEART

Where is the medicine that we are looking for? It is everywhere. Our heart knows where to find it.

Now the question is: do we have our heart in its place? Where is the center of our being? Is it in the open space of the chest? Or is it in the busy head, in the stomach, or in the sexual organs? Where is it?

Now, assuming that our heart is in its place, the next question is: are we using our whole heart? We have heard that one of our great limitations is that we do not use our whole brain. Now let's bring this question to the heart. Do we use our whole heart? One way to know the answer to this question is by observing whether or not our heart is acting as a source of perception. The heart perceives and knows things through deep feelings – much deeper than emotions – and the feelings of the heart are recognitions that happen in the present moment. Aligned to the mind of our spirit, the heart receives pure understanding and wisdom.

I remember a ceremony we did in New Mexico when we were instructed by the Eagle Spirit – one of the mirrors in which we can see an aspect of our sacred nature. He told us that our most urgent task is to recover the other half of our heart. He explained that we are a manipulated humanity needing to awaken its will and to recover its freedom. He also said that we are in a time when we are receiving a great amount of cosmic help to reactivate this part of our heart that went to sleep – a part that some say was stolen from us and others say was brutally repressed.

As we understood it, the Eagle Spirit was referring to the half of our heart that is connected to our spirit, the one in which spiritual visions and dreams dwell. When we are well tuned in, this is the part of our heart where we perceive the presence or absence of truth.

The other half of the heart – the one we normally keep active – is connected to our more human side, our physical, emotional, and mental aspects. This is the half of our heart that tends to our most human need; it makes us love our children and stay busy looking after the well-being of all that is close to us such as home, family, and country. Here I see how our human side and our spiritual side are different: our spiritual side cares for life far beyond what is close to us. Its capacity is so vast that it reaches the well-being of all life.

As most people in modern society have become spiritually asleep and only care for what is immediately related to their human needs, the human race has become careless in relation to the balance of life on Earth and of the universal well-being.

We can also see how living with half a heart affects the capacity for individuals to create a fulfilling life for themselves. One of the reasons it is difficult in these times for most human beings to liberate themselves from the conditions in which they feel trapped is because when they try to do so, they do it half-heartedly. Grandfather Eagle said that today there are only a few spiritual warriors like those of the ancient times. These are the ones who put all their heart into what they do. Without doubting and without conditions they jump into the abyss for what they love, and in the middle of the abyss discover they can fly.

Living with half a heart is allowing doubt and laziness to enter our being after we had already felt with total certainty what we wanted to do – and so we end up not doing it.

Grandfather Eagle explained to us that to live with half a heart severely damages our relationships with all that and all those whom we love. When we love with half a heart, the half of the heart that is absent becomes a place where doubt and selfishness can grow. Afraid of losing something, putting personal interests first, those who live with half a heart remain in conflict with the needs of others, with the common good. As a result, they end up over-protecting their personal interests, separating themselves from others. Once separated, their situation becomes worse. Finding themselves alone and not cooperating with others, explained the Eagle

Spirit, their capacity to make their deepest dreams come true becomes weak. When this capacity becomes weak, they develop the habit of daydreaming, becoming addicted to illusions and fantasies that never manifest.

The Sacred Time of Dreams

Dreams belong to the half of the heart where our awareness of our movement in the time of Spirit lives – a time that is very different from the one of the clock. The speed of time in our dreams is not the same as the speed of ordinary time. It is in our dreams that our heart gets used to welcoming the time of Spirit. This is the magic time with the power to expand the boundaries of our mind, allowing our perception to become closer to spiritual truths charged with a high consciousness and free from human limitations.

Science is also aware of the relativity of time. To put it simply, the study of physics has demonstrated that time cannot be measured by a watch when we get closer to the speed of light or to a black hole. Indigenous people have always known this; when we have experiences in which our spirit's vibration gets closer to the light or to the mystery of a "black hole," time as we normally know it disappears. Every night when going to sleep, we receive the opportunity to have this kind of experience – sometimes in dreams, sometimes in nightmares.

A half a heart is the heart of those who have lost their ability to be fully present in the *dreamtime*. When our presence in the *dreamtime* becomes debilitated, we don't necessarily lose our capacity to dream; what we lose is our conscious connection to dreams. Then we stop receiving the spiritual vibration of our dreams in the receptors of our body's power centers, which weakens our will. This weakness is the incapacity to experience the creative and transformative powers of our spirit while awake. No matter how altruistic or how important the service we are offering to the world seems to be, as long as we remain disconnected from our spiritual source, we are acting with only half of our potential – and not our wisest half. To work in these conditions makes one feel exhausted and sometimes frustrated when, after so much work, nothing seems to have really changed. Even with the help of impressive high-speed technologies at work, these types of feelings continue. The fastest "technology" we can really count on originates in the way we were naturally wired. With our heart connected to the mind of our spirit, we are able to access at the speed of light or in *no time* universal intelligence and compassion. Unfortunately, nowadays this sacred "technology" is not used very much. It still exists in the realm of some remote tribes and monasteries but not in the workplace or people's homes.

Our *Munay* – the will that is born from the heart and charged with the spiritual power of our dreams – is the most precious force we can have. When we do not use this willpower to follow our dreams, we become easy prey for those who sell manufactured dreams. In order to gain the economic power to be able to buy what they sell, we have to stay busy working hard. In order to consume what we buy, even if it is just a television or computer, we have to get busy again. At the end of the day, there is very little time left for some things which are really important, like practices that support our spiritual development or our participation in work that truly helps the world become a better place. Without hours available, without sacred times, without dreams, without will, how can someone have dedication for what is really important?

I believe it is important that we become complete and real human beings. Even when we just prepare a meal for our family, doing it with our full heart is so much better because our "inner medicine" is fully awake. Where is the other half of our heart? Who stole it? Where is it hiding? One answer is the clock. Modern man imprisoned time in the machine, and then became a prisoner of that machine.

Machines are very useful and sometimes even beautiful. The problem is that the pioneers of the industrial world gave the machine the power to keep and guide our time. Since then, most humans live in an artificial reality ruled by a man-made time and deprived of sacred times. In this reality, producing is more important than living. Large numbers of people have become highly productive but have forgotten how to live, how to share their love, how to enjoy life. Living, loving, and enjoying are experiences that need to have their own natural rhythm in order to fully manifest. They need their time and their right timing; but in a world of fixed schedules and full agendas, people have to wait for a vacation to remember how to flow in a natural rhythm. And even when the vacation begins, it is so difficult to be without an agenda! It is difficult to return to a natural rhythm once one has become obedient to an artificial one; but always, after a few days of interrupting our routine, the natural rhythms recorded in the memory of our bodies start coming back.

Should we take our electronic devices with us when we stop our daily routine or leave them at home? Once we put our freedom under the tyranny of the watch, we become easy prey for other machines like the cell phone, computer, and television. Our natural necessity to connect with others finds in these devices the illusion of being connected. Intimacy becomes dependent on having a machine in the middle, and our own inner natural connectors become numb. As a result, we remain afraid and do not grow as we are not challenged by the full presence of other human beings.

The ancient ones were brave. For the ancient ones, the center of their lives was their heart, connected to their dreams and visions. For most people today, the center of their lives is installed in the center of their house or their bedroom: the television, a source of manufactured dreams and visions overloading their minds, handicapping their capacity to generate their own from within.

To observe our dreams is one of the tasks that can help us to wake up. After having a strong dream and becoming aware of it, we often immediately wake up. The dreams that wake us up are the messages of Spirit. The energy of these dreams is a wave that takes us to the shores of waking time, giving us the impulse to walk through a new day without losing the feeling of being a spirit that lives in a magical world.

In relation to this, Grandfather Eagle told us that life is real only when full of magic. He said that, contrary to what most people believe, to live surrounded by magic is what is normal, that the lack of magic is a clear symptom of not having the full heart awake. The natural magic of life, when present, appears constantly in life circumstances – in the places where we are and with the people who we meet. Because magic is a need, the lack of natural magic in people's lives leads them to become intense consumers of the magic of movies and television shows.

The ancient people used their whole heart. They knew how to activate the mind of their spirit and trusted in their dreams; their magic and intelligence built the wonders of the ancient world. They worked in sacred time and at the speed of light when they developed sophisticated knowledge of mathematics, architecture, astronomy, agriculture, medicine, quantum physics, and many other sciences not yet known to modern man. These other sciences, the magic ones, the ones less known, allowed them to lift gigantic stones to build great temples. Their methodology transcended the study of universal laws. They inhabited the laws. They navigated them and loved them with deep gratitude. While becoming one with the universal laws, they fluidly manifested on Earth the fruits of their sacred powers. Then, the communities gathered around these fruits to share them in acts of celebration, nourishing their body and spirit, opening their heart, increasing their compassion, vision and understanding. This was done in large circles in the plazas found next to all the temples of the ancient civilizations. Days and nights they sang and danced, radiating the blessings of the Flowering Earth towards the four directions for the well-being of all life.

These people lived and loved without fear, putting their full heart into all that they did. We carry the genes of these very ancient people within us – all of us come from them.

Sacred time is very necessary for the development of our full heart and our will. This is why Indigenous people make so many ceremonies. Thanks to our ceremonies, we become used to not being slaves of the clock and the machines. We learn to adapt ourselves without fear to mysterious times that are different from the one of the clock.

What happens in ceremony is similar to what happens in dreams. Sometimes, one is aware of falling asleep for five minutes and remembers a dream that in waking time would have taken several hours. For the mind, the dream still feels like it lasted several hours; this doesn't change regardless of what the watch says. Which is the real time? Is it the one that the mind experiences, or the one dictated by the watch? How much longer until the end of time then? It may be different for everyone.

The good news is that many prophecies from around the world speak about the end of time as an experience that will most likely happen soon, at least in our lifetime. This means we are approaching the light or a black hole. The Black Jaguar is here, for sure, getting us ready to "die" and have a clean new start. What else can the end of time be but our liberation from the mental prisons in which we have been trapped?

The Eagle Spirit, who can see far away and has already seen what is coming, has encouraged us to awaken our full heart, to connect not only with our current human needs but also with the vastness that is seen from the mind of our spirit. The equipment we need in order to be ready to meet the end of this time and the birth of the New Earth has clearly been presented to us. We need a big *Munay* vibrating in our chest, we need to become experienced in inhabiting the mystery of sacred time, we need to heal the relationship of the genders so together we may generate new life, we need to accept the guidance that comes from feminine intelligence, we urgently need to put our heart back into our economic system, and most of all, we need to always choose cooperation instead of competition with each other and with Nature. We are singers and dancers, serving Pachamama with our immense capacity to produce the refined vibrations that keep life alive. We are the ones who light the sacred fire, the ones who remember the original songs of Creation. What we see and dream with the mind of our spirit supports the continuity of all life.

LAST SONG

Despite my human limitations, I had dedicated myself to work with my spirit, recovering the ancient memory to share it with others. My dream was that our ancestral nations would occupy their temples again and regain their original way of life. Five hundred years after the Spanish conquest, there was still someone alive in me who had not been conquered – someone waiting for the victory that would come through the truth and the power of Spirit. A deep love united me to the time of our ancestors, and all that I wanted was to make it present again.

Throughout many years, I kept this dream alive until one day I had an experience that changed my perception. It happened while conducting an ancestral ceremony in front of a sacred fire for my people. In an altered state of consciousness, I heard Grandfather Eagle say that this struggle was over. He said that we had no more time left to recover what we lost, and I found myself standing in front of the sacred fire and my people pouring my tears over Pachamama.

Listening to the Eagle Spirit deliver his message in that ceremony, it became clear to me that what our ancestors had built with so much dedication and effort over thousands of years had been severed and would remain incomplete. The damage that was done to our ancient culture could not be reversed in the short time that we had left.

The particular opportunity created by our ancestors for developing a peaceful human race, centered in the heart and in harmony with Nature, was lost. The work of generations was destroyed. What we still have left, more than in the temples, lives in the hearts of the Indigenous communities that keep the memory of the ancient wisdom; it lives in their most simple gestures of generosity, in their tenderness, in their heart-centered way of being. The majority of these communities are threatened by the globalization of high-tech commercial culture, the influence of television, extreme poverty, and alcoholism. They are becoming smaller as the youngsters prefer to move to the big cities to learn the path of competition and success, and so even these remaining communities could also disappear.

But nothing could ever destroy the essential nature of the universe and its gigantic heart, which is a permanent sacred generator of opportunities for all beings. Today I am grateful to the Eagle Spirit for liberating me from my attachment to the old times. His message made me turn and face the opposite direction: the future. Now, I do not only understand but accept that the opportunity that we have is not behind us; it is ahead of us.

I know my dream will come true, but it is not about bringing back the past. It is when I look into the future that I feel hope, foreseeing Pachamama sown with new tribes.

There is no need to defend our race and our culture – this I have accepted. It takes too much energy to be defensive, and defensive attitudes make our ego grow bigger than our heart. Our energy needs to be conserved so that it can be put in service of something more important: the call of the generations to come.

When I see Pachamama becoming once again the fertile ground for the growth of healthy human communities, I don't see this happening exclusively to the actual descendants of Indigenous people. All humans have the right to return home and become indigenous to this Earth, to become real human beings living their full potential as caretakers of life, to become people with big hearts living in coopera-tion with each other and with other forms of life.

Thanks to the power of ceremonies that open our full heart and activate our consciousness, we all can become aware from a young age that for something to become real, there has to be someone to perceive it. Some futures are born from our vision. In the absence of a vision, what remains are the unavoidable consequences of our past actions.

The world that we will pass on to our grandchil-dren is the world that we are capable of dreaming today. To envision a healthy and luminous future is work that we are called to do now, when our Mother Earth is in Her time of renewal. On this very day, the Earth is dying. On this same day, the Earth is pregnant and ready to give birth to a new manifestation of Herself. One of these two possibilities will be nourished to the point of becoming a reality. We are the generation who live in this wonderful time, a time both dangerous and full of opportunities. We don't know if life or death awaits our descendants. Therefore, it is better for us to know what we want.

How beautiful is the moment when two human beings find themselves looking at the same wonder, witnessing a secret that reveals itself in front of their astonished eyes! And what happens when it is not only two people, but three, seven, nine or twelve? What happens when the visionaries start living together around their visions? What kind of home is this?

A common-unity has been born. In time, they will have descendants, and they will be called a tribe. Women, men, and children will feed themselves from the fruits of a new tree. The mysterious power of life will find a path for its continuity in the veins of the humans, and the humans, full of this energy, will love the Earth and all Her creatures.

At these times of renewal of life on Earth, new designs, new life, and new tribes are being animated. We who are here now are being invited to come closer to the center and take a look at what's happening there. We are invited to come closer to the heart where colorful seeds of life are germinating and radiant designs are looking for a path to manifest their physical existence. When these lights come through us and move us to do something, it is good to do it without allowing our doubts to interfere. It is the essence of life that is seeking to continue living and multiplying itself through us, the human race.

.

GLOSSARY

Apukuna: Spirits of the Mountains *(Runasimi)*.

Andean People: Inhabitants of the areas in and around the Andes in South America.

Ayni: Reciprocity *(Runasimi)*.

Hanblecheyapi: The ceremony of Crying for a Dream or Vision, also known as a Vision Quest (Lakota).

Haywarikuy: To hand something to someone with tenderness *(Runasimi)*.

Lakota: An Indigenous tribe of North America. Can also refer to the Lakota language.

Munay: Love, wanting, the heart's power, the heart's will *(Runasimi)*.

Pacha: Time, Space, Universe *(Runasimi)*.

Pachamama: Mother Earth, Mother of Time, Mother of the Universe. *(Runasimi)*.

Pachacamaq: The Spirit that animates the world made out of time and space *(Runasimi).*

Runasimi: The language of the Indigenous people of the Andes. Runa means people. Simi means language. Also known as Quechua.

Taku Wakan Skan Skan: Something that is Sacred Energy in Permanent Motion *(Lakota).*

Tiospaye: Extended Family, Community *(Lakota).*

Tukuy Sonkoy: With all the heart *(Runasimi).*

Wakan Tanka: The Great Sacred Energy *(Lakota).*

Waka: A place where the Great Sacred Energy dwells *(Runasimi).*

Wambli: Eagle *(Lakota).*

Wopila: Gratitude *(Lakota).*

Made in the USA
San Bernardino, CA
11 December 2012

is the Bible
a jigsaw Puzzle...

is the Bible a jigsaw Puzzle...

An evaluation of Hal Lindsey's writings

by

T. Boersma

PAIDEIA PRESS
St. Catharines, Ontario, Canada

First published in Dutch as *De Bijbel is geen puzzelboek*.
© J. Boersma B.V. of Enschede. Translated by Elizabeth
Vanderkooy Roberts.

ISBN 0-88815-019-9
Printed in the United States of America.